The Deacon in the Church

alba house

DIVISION OF THE SOCIETY OF ST. PAUL
2187 VICTORY BLVD.
STATEN ISLAND, N.Y. 10314

THE DEACON

IN

THE CHURCH

Past and Future

Edward P. Echlin, S.J.

Nihil Obstat
    Daniel V. Flynn, J.C.D.
    Censor Librorum

Imprimatur
    Joseph P. O'Brien, S.T.D.
    Vicar General, Archdiocese of New York
    March 16, 1971

The nihil obstat and imprimatur are official declarations that a book or pamphlet is free of doctrinal or moral error. No implication is contained therein that those who have granted the nihil obstat and imprimatur agree with the contents, opinions or statements expressed.

Library of Congress Catalog Card Number 75-158571

Designed, printed and bound in the U.S.A. by the Pauline Fathers and Brothers of the Society of St. Paul, 2187 Victory Blvd., Staten Island, N.Y. 10314 as part of their communications apostolate.

to my parents

Contents

Contents

Introduction

"THESE LORDS MAY LIGHT THE MYSTERY
OF MASTERY OR VICTORY,
AND THESE RIDE HIGH IN HISTORY,
BUT THESE SHALL NOT RETURN."

"THE BALLAD OF THE WHITE HORSE"
G. K. CHESTERTON

After the lapse of a millennium the permanent deacon, un-like the thanes of Alfred's England, has returned to the Latin west.

The deacon returns to his ministry in an age when men have rediscovered their radical historicity, a discovery that, paradoxi-cally, casts the long shadow of doubt on the value of research into the past. If the world is not fixed but in process, what is to be learned from riders of forgotten yesterdays who shall never return? If the future course of the human biography is man's task what point is there in bending above shapeless shrouds and forgotten clay? If golden ages of the past will never return should not Christians confine themselves to the abundant challenges of the present and future?

This book proceeds from the conviction that while the future indeed lies open, indispensable light for man's future path is to be found in the musty shadows of the past. Specifically, we shall not adequately discern the future deacon, unless we know something of the deacon who once was. Within the dis-continuities of the historical process the diaconate will develop in substantial continuity with the diaconate of yesterday. His-tory, therefore, still holds enormous treasure for human self-understanding. Every man is concerned about what happened to a little boy. We can avoid pitfalls that ensnared our ancestors, and we can succeed where they succeeded, if we discern the lessons of history. God's people can best welcome the returning deacons into their communities if they know something about his family background.

After the lapse of a millennium the deacon's role is shadowy indeed. Despite the sudden reappearance of these men as special ministers at liturgy, word and charity, God's people are asking who and what they are and whence they come. When did they decline? Why restore them? What can they do that priests and laity cannot? This book, by offering a sketch of the deacon who once was and then was not, is an attempt to assist God's people in answering these questions.

At Vatican II God's people, gathered in the ecumenical council, restored the permanent diaconate to the Roman Communion. And like so many decisions, taken in a council when the Spirit's guidance is intensified, the full meaning of this dramatic restoration will be discerned as the diaconate develops.

The deacon of the past was official mediator of Christian reconciliation. Because the Mother Church and the world it serves yearn for human reconciliation the restored diaconate should be warmly received. The deacon who once was witnessed in his person to the human community that Christianity yearns to establish. He was, and again is, a sign to all men of what all men are called to be.

The origins of the deacon who once was may be discovered in the origins of Christian ministry. As the triadic ministry developed so did the diaconate. In the pre-Nicene era his ministry flourished in a golden age of diaconal mediation. But with the rise of sacerdotalism when "old presbyters became new priests" the diaconate declined until, by the tenth century, it was almost everywhere in the west a preliminary step to the priesthood. The Council of Trent attempted to restore the primitive diaconal functions, but not until Vatican II did the Roman Church revive the permanent diaconate. Today Christian ministry and the world it serves are the richer as deacons rejoin priests and bishops in service of the human family.

The future deacon and those he serves will best adapt to tomorrow's challenges by familiarizing themselves with the deacon who once was. The past deacon rides high in history, lighting the mystery of mastery and victory. These pages look to the past not for the past's sake, but with an eye to the future of the once and future deacon.

Edward P. Echlin

John Carroll University
December 26, 1970
Feast of St. Stephen

The Origins
of the Diaconate

The origins of the permanent diaconate cannot be studied in isolation, but must be discovered within the development of the apostolic ministry of bishop, presbyter, and deacon.[1] The diaconate developed gradually as the Church structured its ministry to meet the needs of the new people of God and of the whole human family.

Robert Nowell cautions us against looking to the apostolic Church for the fully developed diaconate: "The difficulty comes really from forgetting that the early Church was an organic growth: we are apt to expect to find already precisely formulated at a very primitive stage structures and offices that only developed gradually in response to circumstances and needs. It seems safer to start from the assumption that the diaconate developed gradually." [2] In the first century the Church struggled to structure its ministry until, after a very complex development, the Catholic order of bishop, presbyter, and deacon prevailed.[3]

In structuring the diaconal function the early Church looked to the institutions of Judaism. In the Old Testament there was a striking connection between worship and service of the neigh-

---

1. Hans Küng, *The Church*, New York, 1968, pp. 363-444.
2. Robert Nowell, *The Ministry of Service*, London, 1968, pp. 40-41.
3. Myles Bourke, "Presidential Address," *The Catholic Biblical Quarterly*, Spring, 1968, pp. 493-511.

3

bor, between *leiturgia* and *diaconia* (Dt 14:26-29; 2 S 6:19). It is understandable, then, that in early Christian writings *leiturgia* connoted both worship and service of the neighbor.[4] Significantly, St. Paul reprimanded wealthy Corinthians for not sharing with the poor when the Church at Corinth gathered for worship (1 Cor 11). The letter of James calls the service of widows and orphans "pure, untainted religion," cultic words that connect both worship and charity (Jm 1:27). In structuring its ministry the early Church developed the permanent diaconate as a special sign and agent of the connection between Christian liturgy and service of the deprived.

The early Church frequently compared the diaconal function to the ministry of the post-exilic Jewish levites. When the temples at Bethel and Jerusalem attracted people from the lesser shrines the levites became assistants to the temple priests, helpers to the sons of Aaron (Ez 24:6; Nb 3:6-9). Levites served God's people as doorkeepers, administrators, chanters, and custodians of vessels and loaves. Although circumstances after the exile made their role subordinate to that of other priests, levites were supported by the people. They continued to teach and to serve. The similarity between Jewish levites and Christian deacons is striking,[5] and early Christian writers made use of this comparison in describing the role of deacons.

In pre-Christian literature, including the septuagint version of the Old Testament, *diakonos, diakonein,* and *diakonia* re-

---

4. Jean Paul Audet may exaggerate the independence of Christian ministry from Judaism in *Structures of Christian Priesthood*, New York, 1967, pp. 77-85.

5. Gregory Dix, "The Ministry in the Early Church," in *The Apostolic Ministry*, K. E. Kirk, ed., London, 1962.

ferred to service, especially the menial service of assistance at tables.[6] Christ used these words to describe his ministry and that of his disciples: "Whoever would be great among you must be your servant (*diakonos*)... even as the Son of Man did not come to be served but to serve and give his life as a ransom for many" (Mt 20:26; par.). Christian ministry, therefore, is service.

While the New Testament refers to all Christian ministry as *diakonia,* even the earliest writings begin to designate certain leaders of the community as *diakonoi* or servants in a special sense. In other words, as the Church gradually structured its ministry certain Christians were designated *diakonoi*: but in a general sense all baptized Christians, including church officers, were *diakonoi.* The division of special *diakonoi* from the college of *presbyteroi* or leading elders and, in the Pauline churches, from other gifted servants developed gradually. It is anachronistic to read into apostolic Church order the fully developed diaconate of the second century.

In the apostolic age the Church ordered its ministry to provide special services that differed from the services of the apostles, presbyters, prophets, and teachers. These were the services that permanent deacons eventually gave. In Paul's letter to the Romans he praises a servant who performed a special diaconal function, and that servant was a deaconess named Phoebe. Paul's praise of Phoebe indicates that the diaconal function was developing. His warm words about Phoebe's services also demonstrate he valued the role of women

---

6. Jean Colson, *La Fonction Diaconale Aux Origines De L'Eglise,* Paris, 1960, pp. 9-10.

in the Church.[7] "I commend to you our sister Phoebe, a deaconess of the Church at Cenchreae. Give her, in union with the Lord, a welcome worthy of the saints. She has looked after a great many people, myself included" (Rm 16:1-2).

Phoebe's services for Paul and a "great many people" were primarily services of charity. Her role was that of Christ at Passover worship washing his disciples' feet. When Paul was travelling he depended on the services of women like Phoebe to deliver his letters, provide food and shelter and a place for the liturgy and in some cases literally to wash the feet of visitors. Already with Phoebe we observe *diakonos* being applied to persons who looked after the basic needs of liturgy and charity. The Gentile churches were structuring the diaconal function at a very early date.

But the classical text in scripture for the origins of the diaconate is the account in Acts of the appointment of seven hellenists to serve at the tables of Jerusalem widows. Hellenist Jews who were resident in Jerusalem complained that their widows were neglected at the daily ministration to the needy. The twelve responded by calling a meeting of the community. The assembly chose seven hellenists and presented them to the twelve who "ordained" them for the daily ministration to hellenist widows.

About this time when the number of disciples was increasing the hellenists made a complaint against the Hebrews. In the daily distribution their own widows were being over-

---

7. *The Jerusalem Bible*, Alexander Jones, ed., New York, 1967, p. 290, note.

looked. So the twelve called a full meeting of the disciples and addressed them, 'It would not be right for us to neglect the Word of God so as to give out food. You, brothers, must select from among yourselves seven men of good reputation filled with the Spirit and with wisdom. We will hand over this duty to them and continue to devote ourselves to prayer and to the service of the Word.' The whole assembly approved of this proposal and elected Stephen, a man full of faith and of the Holy Spirit, together with Philip, Prochorus, Nicanor, Timon, Parmenas and Nicolaus of Antioch, a convert to Judaism. They presented these to the apostles who prayed and laid their hands on them (Acts 6:1-6).

What makes the ordering of the seven for diaconal function so important is that it demonstrates how the apostolic Church responded to the "need for a structure of the community." [8] Since the time of Irenaeus Christian writings have anachronistically referred to the ordering of the seven as the institution of the permanent diaconate. It is more accurate to see here the Church structuring its ministry but not the ordination of officers clearly differentiated from other community leaders.

Stephen and his companions complained not because there were no officers at Jerusalem to feed the poor but because the *hellenist* widows were neglected. Those commissioned to feed the poor were slighting the widows of Greek-speaking Jews. If

---

8. Richard J. Dillon and Joseph A. Fitzmyer, "Acts of the Apostles," in *The Jerome Biblical Commentary*, Raymond Brown, ed., Englefield Cliffs, 1968, p. 181. Cf. also Lukas Vischer, "The Ministry of Deacons," in *The Ministry of Deacons*, Geneva, 1965, p. 20.

Jerusalem presbyters were responsible for the daily ministration, there was an early rift in the love community which Luke glosses over.

Another reason for caution in referring to the seven as "deacons" in the clearly defined meaning of that office is that Stephen and Philip continued to preach and baptize, functions customarily performed at that time by the apostles and presbyters (Acts 6:8; 8:5). But structuring was admittedly underway. The apostles, for example, performed their own specific services such as the imposition of hands on the seven, the normative preaching of the word, and in Samaria the liturgical imposition of hands on neophytes (Acts 8:14, 17). The Church has repeatedly returned to the appointment of the seven in determining the diaconal function. Vatican II did not depart from this tradition although the fathers realized that the seven were not as clearly differentiated from presbyters as were the permanent deacons of the second century.[9]

The reason why the apostles appointed the seven to serve the poor has singular importance for the ministry of the secular age. The apostles, whose primary service was ministry of the word, were loathe to infringe on that ministry by serving at tables. Social work would have distracted them from effective preaching and prayer. Yet ministration to the poor was so important that they gathered the community to elect seven men for this daily task; but for the apostles themselves, *diakonia logou,* ministry of the word, was of paramount importance. The priest

---

9. Joseph Lécuyer, "Les Diacres Dans Le Nouveau Testament," in *Le Diacre Dans L'Eglise Et Le Monde D'Aujourd'hui,* P. Winninger and Y. Congar, eds., Paris, 1966, p. 19.

of the secular age and the people he serves can discern what the priest's role should be by reflecting on *the reason why* the twelve appointed the seven to serve at tables.[10]

In Paul's church at Philippi there were church officers called *diakonoi* or deacons. Paul greets them as well as the *episcopoi* (bishops-presbyters) in his letter to the Philippians. "From Paul and Timothy, servants of Christ Jesus, to all the saints in Christ, together with their presiding *episcopoi* and *diakonoi,* we wish you the grace and peace of God our Father and of the Lord Jesus Christ" (Ph 1:1).

We notice that deacons enjoyed roles of leadership at Philippi and that they were closely associated with *episcopoi.* But Paul gives us no more explicit information about these officers, nor does he mention them elsewhere in the four letters definitely attributed to him. We cannot presume that the diaconate was clearly differentiated from the episcopal-presbyteral college when Paul wrote to Philippi (A.D. 57). It is noteworthy, however, that when the diaconate *was* fully developed in Asia Minor fifty years later, deacons, as at Paul's Philippi, were closely associated with other officers and they too were to be obeyed by the people. Ordering was underway when Paul greeted the *episcopoi* and *diakonoi* at Philippi.

In the same letter Paul praises a minister named Epaphroditus for the assistance he had rendered the apostle. Epaphroditus may have been one of the deacons. "He was sent as your representative to help me when I needed someone to be my companion in working and battling . . . people like him are

---

10. Myles Bourke, "The Catholic Priest, Man of God for Others," *Worship,* Vol. 43, pp. 68-81.

to be honored. It was for Christ's work that he came so near to dying, and he risked his life to give me the help that you were not able to give me yourselves" (Ph 2:25-30). At a minimum Paul's greeting to different officers with different titles and his praise of Epaphroditus for help and companionship indicate that the diaconal function was gradually being structured even in the Pauline churches.

This structuring is more evident in the letter to Timothy (A.D. 65) which gives directions for the organization of the local community. The author enumerates the qualities to be expected of *episcopoi* and *diakonoi*. The residential mono-episcopate had yet to develop, for the author addresses *episcopoi* and presbyters interchangeably.

We learn something about the developing diaconate when the author of 1 Timothy spells out the desired qualifications for aspirants to this office.

> Deacons must be respectable men whose word can be trusted, moderate in the amount of wine they drink and with no squalid greed for money. They must be conscientious believers in the mystery of the faith. They are to be examined first and only admitted to serve as deacons if there is nothing against them. In the same way the women must be respectable, not gossips but sober and reliable. Deacons must not have been married more than once, and must be men who manage their children and family well. Those of them who carry out their duties well as deacons will earn a high standing for themselves and be rewarded with great assurance for their work for the faith in Christ Jesus (1 Tm 3:8-13).

Both *episcopoi* and deacons were elected from respected men in the community. This indicates that deacons were important persons in the early Church. Their comportment and reputation had to correspond to the importance of their office.

The letter to Timothy requires that deacons be men of their word, a requirement that is *not* mentioned explicitly in the list of qualifications for *episcopoi* (1 Tm 3:1-7; Tt 1:6-9). This may indicate that deacons were already acting as mediators who represented the episcopal voice to the people and who reported the needs of the people to the *episcopoi*.

The necessity of sobriety is understandable from what we know about the functions of the seven hellenists. Deacons brought bread and wine to the tables of the poor.

Episcopoi and deacons were to be free from attachment to wealth. As community leaders these officers would have had some responsibility for administration of the community's resources. We know from Acts that church officers took responsibility for distribution of goods to the poor.

Recently it has been suggested that the famous Pauline strictures against remarriage may mean that ministers should be totally loyal to their wives.[11] Paul does accept a *married* ministry and even recommends that young widows *remarry* (1 Tm 5:14). But his prohibition of remarriage for older women who were enrolled in the order of widows bolsters the traditional interpretation that for Paul it was better for ministers to burn than remarry.

---

11. Audet suggests that instead of interpreting Paul as opposed to remarriage in the ministry we may surmise that he means a minister must be "undividedly attached to his wife." Cf. Audet, *Structures of Christian Priesthood*, pp. 57-61.

Deacons and *episcopoi* were to be successful husbands and fathers. Paul develops this qualification more at length for *episcopoi* than for deacons. This in itself is significant. It was primarily the *episcopoi* who were responsible for leading the community. And if these men could not manage their own wives and children, how could they lead God's people? Of bishops and not of deacons Paul asks, "How can any man who does not understand how to manage his own family. have responsibility for the church of God?" (1 Tm 3: 5). Deacons did not manage the church but gave special services.

At the church of Ephesus there was an order of deaconesses, valuable women who were "respectable, not gossips but sober and reliable." Deaconesses were not merely "spouses" of deacons and *episcopoi* as some medieval writers were to contend,[12] but servants of the church of God. They served in communion with an order of widows who were distinct from "young" widows on the one hand and deaconesses on the other. Paul's exigitive requirements for admission to this order seem to indicate that he had more in mind than enrollment in the community's welfare program.[13]

Enrollment as a widow is permissible only for a woman at least sixty years old who has had only one husband. She must be a woman known for her good works and for the way in which she has brought up her children, shown hospitality to strangers and washed the saints' feet, helped people who are in trouble and been active in all sorts of good works. Do not accept young widows because if their

---

12. Colson, *La Fonction Diaconal,* p. 64, note 1.
13. *Ibid.,* pp. 65-67.

natural desires get stronger than their dedication to Christ they want to remarry and then people condemn them for being unfaithful to their original promise . . . (1 Tm 5:9-13).

By including women in the ordering of the church God's people enriched the diaconal function and added a dimension to Christian service that no man could render. As Jean Colson remarks, "In certain cases, such as caring for the needs of women, and for certain care where nothing can substitute for a woman's hand and maternal concern, it was desirable that these roles be filled by women of experience, such as mature widows of proven conduct." [14]

But Paul and his surrogates were reluctant to admit women to ministry of the word. In the first letter to Corinth Paul tells women in no uncertain terms to keep quiet during assemblies: "As in all the churches of the saints women are to keep quiet at meetings since they have no permission to speak; they must keep in the background as the Lord himself lays it down. If they have any questions to ask, they should ask their husbands at home; it does not seem right for a woman to raise her voice at meetings" (1 Cor 14:34-35). In the letter to Timothy which clearly welcomes a role for women in the church we come up against the same reluctance to let women speak in the assembly: "During instructions a woman should be quiet and respectful. I am not giving permission for a woman to teach or to tell a man what to do" (1 Tm 2:11 cf. 1 Cor 11, 5, 10).

Women ministered to human needs in the Gentile churches. But Paul's cultural heritage and his exegesis of Genesis com-

---

14. *Ibid.*, p. 67.

pelled him to draw back from admitting women to roles of
leading and preaching. Paul did not answer many of the questions being asked about women today. We cannot expect him
to answer questions he was never asked. He did recommend
a role for women in the ordering of the community. His reluctance to admit them to a complete share in the ministry of
episcopoi and deacons is not normative for our times when the
Church is structured differently than were the churches of Paul
and when Christians are asking different questions than were
asked of the apostle.

Within a generation after Paul's death there was serious
friction about the church's ministry at Corinth.[15] The letter
of Clement, a leading Roman presbyter, reveals that the Corin-
thian church had eventually structured itself by appointing
presbyters (*or episcopoi*) and deacons. But trouble erupted and
a cabal of Corinthians deposed these ministers. To reconcile
the various factions Clement wrote his letter calling for unity
with the presbyters and deacons.

Clement exhorted the Corinthians to *order*. In an analogy
that was itself to provoke controversy in future centuries Clement compared Church order to the order in the Jewish hierarchy. Clement does not explicitly compare Church order
to Jewish priesthood. His concern is not to sacralize the primitive ministry but to restore order in the Church. However,
his mention of Jewish levites as the order just before the laity

---

15. Joannes Quasten, *Patrology*, Vol. 1, Westminster, 1940, p. 49;
cf. Colson, *L'Eveque*, pp. 67-75; Maxwell Stamforth observes that 1
Clement is "the earliest and most valuable surviving example of Christian
literature outside the New Testament," in *Early Christian Writings*,
Maxwell Stamforth, ed., Baltimore, 1968, p. 17.

is important because of the use the later Church will make of the comparison in determining the role of deacons. "Special functions are assigned to the high priest; a special office is imposed upon the priests; and special ministrations fall to the levites. The layman is bound by the rules laid down for the laity" (1 Clement 40).[16]

Taking liberties with the complex origins of the ministry and accommodating scripture to his purposes, Clement argues that the apostles appointed their first converts *episcopoi* and deacons, as scripture "somewhere" had foretold:

> From their earliest converts [the apostles] appointed men whom they had tested by the Spirit to act as bishops and deacons for the future believers. And this was no innovation, for, a long time before the scripture had spoken about bishops and deacons; for somewhere it says, ' I will establish their overseers in observance of the law and their ministers in fidelity' (1 Clement 42; cf. Is 60:17).

The role of these ministers was *leiturgia,* service in worship and in charity.[17] Clement was concerned mainly with the ministry of the bishops (presbyters) but since deacons were associated with them both in their ministry and in their expulsion, we may conclude that the diaconal function involved ministry of liturgy and charity.

---

16. Clement of Rome, "The First Epistle to the Corinthians," in *The Epistles of St. Clement of Rome and St. Ignatius of Antioch,* James Kleist, ed., (Ancient Christian Writers) Westminster, 1949, p. 33.

17. Kleist remarks that "each official is to offer the gifts (*dora*) that belong to his *sacred* ministry." *Ibid.,* pp. 112-113, (italics added).

... we cannot think it right for these men now to be ejected from their ministry, when, after being commissioned by the apostles (or by other reputable persons at a later date) with the full consent of the Church, they have since been serving Christ's flock in a humble, peaceable, and disinterested way, and earning everybody's approval over so long a period of time (1 Clement 44).

The *Didache* corroborates the evidence in 1 Clement that deacons were functioning in the late first century and that their function was *leiturgia*. In its present form the *Didache* is an early Church order that may have been compiled as late as 150, but the norms for polity derive from sources extending back into the first century.

The *Didache* orders the appointment of *episcopoi* and deacons who perform the same ministry (*leiturgian*) as travelling prophets and teachers. There was, therefore, a plurality of ordering well into the late first century. Only with difficulty did *episcopoi* and deacons supplant prophets and teachers.

Appoint for yourselves, then, bishops and deacons who are worthy of the Lord — men who are unassuming and not greedy, who are honest and have been proved. For they also are performing for you the task of the prophets and teachers. Therefore, do not hold them in contempt, for they are honorable men among you, along with the prophets and teachers (15:1-2).[18]

---

18. Robert A. Kraft, *The Apostolic Fathers, A Translation and Commentary*, Vol. 3, *The Didache and Barnabas*, 6 Vols., Toronto, 1965, pp. 76-77.

Deacons did by reason of their office what prophets and teachers did by reason of *their* charism which was itself becoming institutionalized. The task of prophets and teachers, and therefore of *episcopoi* and deacons, was to preach (1 Cor 12:10), to serve the community (1 Cor 14:14), to teach, encourage, reprove, correct and console (1 Cor 14:3). By preaching the mystery of Christ (1 Cor 13:2) they brought men to the faith (Rm 16:26).

In the *Didache* we observe again the early Church's concern, which will continue to manifest itself, that deacons be honest men. Deacons clearly assisted in administration and distribution of money. They were men of integrity "who are unassuming and not greedy, who are honest and have been proved" (15:2).

Another early second century document, the *Shepherd of Hermas,* reveals that ordering proceeded more gradually at Rome than in the churches of the Pastorals. This anonymous Jewish-Christian writing, probably compiled near Rome, occasionally refers to Church officers *in globo* as presbyters (3 Vis. 1:8; 5:1; 9:7).[19]

But in a vision the author saw deacons among the main stones of a building that is the Church.[20]

The stones that are fair and white and fit their joints are the apostles and bishops and teachers and deacons who have walked according to the holiness of God and who

---

19. A good translation of Hermas is Graydon Snyder, *The Apostolic Fathers, A New Translation and Commentary,* Vol. 6, *The Shepherd of Hermas,* 6 Vols., Toronto, 1968.

20. *Ibid.,* pp. 46-47, note. Cf. E. Schweizer, *Church Order in the New Testament,* London, 1961, p. 159.

have sincerely and reverently served the elect of God as bishops and teachers and deacons (3 Vis. 5:1).

In a parable, possibly dating from the second century, we learn that the Church had good reason for its concern that deacons be honest. Some deacons "served badly" by robbing widows and orphans.

The ones with blemishes are deacons who served badly and stole the livelihood of widows and orphans and profited for themselves from the service which they received to perform. If, then, they persist in the same desire they are dead and there is no hope of life for them. But if they turn and sincerely complete their service they will be able to live (Sim. 9:26, 2).

The widows and orphans in question were sheltered by bishops in their homes, another indication of the association of deacons with the leading church officials (Sim. 9:27, 2). When Catholic order is fully developed deacons will serve in communion with the bishop.[21]

And in the brief, dramatic letters of Ignatius of Antioch we meet the fully developed order Catholics know so well — bishop, presbyters, and deacons.[22] When Ignatius and his party halted at Smyrna, some Ephesian Christians, led by their bishop Onesimus, journeyed the forty miles to greet the renowned

21. Cf. supra, pp. 8-9.
22. A good translation of the letters of Ignatius and Polycarp is Maxwell Stamforth's *Early Christian Writings,* pp. 75-123.

bishop of Antioch. In a letter to all the Ephesians Ignatius asked
if he could keep as his companion the Ephesian deacon named
Burrhus.

> Now, about my fellow-servitor Burrhus, whom God has
> made your deacon and endowed with every blessing. Might
> I ask you to let him remain here with me, that would do
> honor both to you and to your bishop (Eph 2).

The request was promptly granted. The churches at Ephesus
and Smyrna raised money to support Burrhus in his service
as companion and secretary to Ignatius.

Ignatius also responded to the visit of some Magnesian
Christians by sending a letter to the church in that city. He
praised the deacon Zotion for his deference to his young bishop
and the presbyters.

> It was my privilege to have a glimpse of you in the persons
> of your saintly bishop Damas and his two clergy, the worthy
> Bassus and Apollonius, as well as my fellow servitor Zotion
> the deacon. I should be happy in that man's company; he
> is as deferential to his bishop as he is to the grace of God,
> and to his clergy as to the law of Jesus Christ (Magn. 2).

Ignatius calls deacons his "fellow-servitors" an encomium
he does not render to presbyters. Deacons, his "special friends,"
were associated with him in service of the community.

And his paramount concern was Christian *unity*. Unity
was assured by union with the triadic ministry in which dea-

cons were compared to Christ. "Let the bishop preside in the place of God, and clergy in place of the apostolic conclave, and let my special friends the deacons be entrusted with the service of Jesus Christ" (Magn. 6).

In his letter to Tralles Ignatius reminds the community the deacons are not only ministers of food and drink. They are servants of the Church of God.

> The deacons too who serve the mystery of Jesus Christ must be men universally approved in every way; since they are not mere dispensers of meat and drink, but servants of the church of God, and therefore under obligation to guard themselves against any slur or imputation as strictly as they would against fire itself (Trall. 2).

Obedience to the triadic ministry was the lynchpin of a united community. The bishop was the head, the presbyters the council, the deacons servants of God's Church. Ignatius adds that deacons are to be respected as Jesus Christ.

> It is for the rest of you to hold the deacon in as great respect as Jesus Christ; just as you should also look on the bishop as a type of the Father, and the presbyters as the apostolic circle forming his council, for without these three orders no church has any right to the name (Trall. 3).

After departing from Smyrna Ignatius headed for Troas by way of Philadelphia. He visited briefly with the Philadelphian Christians and later, from Troas, wrote them a farewell letter.

His favorite refrain of unity with the ministry appears in the opening greeting. "I send you greetings in the Blood of Jesus Christ, wherein is joy eternal and unfailing; all the more so when men are at one with their bishop — and with their clergy and deacons too" (Ph 4).

There was one eucharist just as there was one ministry. From the context we may conclude that deacons were ministers in *liturgy*.

There is but one Body of our Lord Jesus Christ, and but one cup of union with his blood, and one single altar of sacrifice — even also as there is but one bishop with his clergy and my own fellow-servitors the deacons, this will ensure that all your doings are in full accord with the word of God (Ph 4).

Deacons were ministers of the *word*. "Philo the deacon from Cilicia who has been so well spoken of, is at present giving me his help in preaching God's word" (Ph 11).

Deacons were also bearers of letters between the churches, a ministry of *charity*.

It would therefore be very fitting for you as a church of God to appoint one of your deacons to go there (Antioch) as God's ambassador, and when they are all assembled together to offer them your felicitations and to give glory to the Name (Ph 10). The brethren here at Troas send you their love and greetings. That is where I am writing this; and it will come to you by the hand of Burrhus whom the Ephesians and Smyrnians sent to bear me company, as a mark of honor (Ph 11).

In a letter to his former hosts at Smyrna Ignatius warns against any eucharist not celebrated by the bishop or his delegate. We cannot be certain what person a bishop delegated for the presidency. Ignatius also warns against baptism and agape conducted without his sanction. Considering the importance of deacons within Ignatian ecclesiology we cannot exclude the possibility that "the person authorized" to celebrate the eucharist may on occasion have been a deacon.

Follow your bishop, every one of you, as obediently as Jesus Christ followed the Father. Obey your clergy, too, as you would the apostles; give your deacons the same reverence that you would to a command from God. Make sure that no step affecting the Church is ever taken without the bishop's sanction. The sole Eucharist you should consider valid is one that is celebrated by the bishop himself, or by some person authorized by him. Where the bishop is to be seen, there let all the people be; just as wherever Jesus Christ is present, we have the worldwide Church. Nor is it permissible to conduct baptisms or love-feasts without the bishop. On the other hand whatever does have his sanction can be sure of God's approval too. This is the way to make sure of the soundness and validity of anything you do (Smyrn. 8).

The letter to Smryna was delivered by the Ephesian deacon Burrhus, a fellow-servitor for whom Ignatius had great praise.

This letter comes to you from Troas by the hand of Burrhus, whom you and the brethren of Ephesus have jointly sent as a companion for me. He has been the greatest solace to me in every way; I wish that everyone else could be like him, for he is the perfect pattern of the sacred ministry, and the favor of God will surely reward him richly. My greetings to your sainted bishop, to the reverend clergy, to my fellow-servitors the deacons, and each and every one of you in the Name of Jesus Christ (Smyrn. 12).

In the letter to Smyrna Ignatius sent special greetings to women. "Greetings too to the families of my brethren who have wives and children, and to those virgins whom you call widows" (13). If the "virgins called widows" were an order of women they would have served at least by prayer in communion with deacons. They do not play an important role in Ignatian church order, for only in the letter to Smyrna does he mention them. But the fact that he does mention them shows his recognition of a role for women in the church.

In a letter to Polycarp Ignatius again calls for obedience to the triadic ministry. Deacons too were to be obeyed.

Pay careful regard to your bishop if you wish God to pay regard to you. My heart warms to men who are obedient to their bishop and presbyters and deacons, and I pray for a place in heaven at their side (To Polycarp, 6).

Polycarp himself wrote a letter to Philippi in which we notice again the early Church's concern that deacons be honest. Another recurrent theme is the comparison of deacons to Christ the servant.

Our deacons must never be open to any reproach at the bar of his righteousness, remembering that they are ministers of God and not of men. There must be no traducing of others, no paltering of the truth, no itching palms; they must be men utterly self-disciplined, humane and hardworking, who pass their lives in the true spirit of the Lord who came to be the servant of us all (Polycarp, 5).

Polycarp singles out the deacons when exhorting the Philippians to purity, "Our younger men, like the deacons, must be unspotted in all respects, making purity their first care and keeping a strict curb on any tendencies to loose living." The Philippians are exhorted to avoid all carnal vices and to obey the presbyters and deacons. "Our duty, therefore, is to give everything of this kind a very wide berth, and be as obedient to our clergy and deacons as we should be to God and Christ" (*Ibid.*).

In remarks directed to widows Polycarp compares these women to an altar of God. That is, they received the offerings of the community and, in turn, offered prayers for the community. Neither he nor Ignatius testify to an order of deaconesses.

Widows are to observe discretion as they practice the Lord's faith; they should make constant intercession for everyone, and be careful to avoid all tale-bearing, spiteful tittle-tattle, false allegations, over-eagerness for money, or misconduct of any description. They are to recognize that they are an altar of God, who scrutinizes every offering laid on it (4).

Conclusion

In scripture and the non-canonical writings of the late first century we see the Church structuring the diaconal function. It is anachronistic to look to the apostolic church for the clearly structured ministry of later centuries. However, there was from the start a recognition by the Church that there was a need for designated men and women to provide particular services of liturgy, word, and charity in close cooperation with other Church officers.

At the turn of the century in Syria and Asia Minor the triadic ministry of bishop, presbyters, and deacons is clearly manifest in the letters of Ignatius of Antioch and Polycarp of Smyrna. Within the context of liturgy, word, and charity permanent deacons worked in close communion with the bishop. In the pre-Nicene period permanent deacons flourished in a golden age of diaconal service, until in the fourth century with the rise of sacerdotalism the gradual decline of the permanent diaconate began.

From Ignatius to Nicea: The Golden Age

In the two centuries from Ignatius to Nicea permanent deacons were vitally important ministers of the Church. Their ministry was as much a part of Church order as was the ministry of bishops and presbyters. In fact at small country churches deacons occasionally assisted the presiding bishop without the ministrations of presbyters. At second century Rome Justin Martyr described the eucharistic ministry of deacons who distributed the elements to the assembly and conveyed communion to absent brethren.

At the end of these prayers and thanksgiving, all present express their approval by saying 'Amen.' This Hebrew word 'Amen' means 'So be it.' And when he who presides has celebrated the eucharist they whom we call deacons permit each one present to partake of the Eucharistic bread, and wine and water; and they convey it also to the absentees (First Apology, 65, cf. 67).[1]

In his brilliant treatise *Against Heresies* Irenaeus of Lyons refers only in passing to deacons. His fleeting references are significant for two reasons: 1) they reveal that deacons served

---

1. Justin Martyr, "First Apology" in *Saint Justin Martyr*, Thomas Falls, ed., (The Fathers of the Church), N. Y., 1948, p. 105.

not only in Syria, Asia Minor, and Rome, but in southern Gaul as well; and, 2) Irenaeus inaugurates a tradition which continues even today of tracing the origins of the diaconate to the appointment of the seven hellenists. He praises Stephen "who was chosen the first deacon by the apostles, and who, of all men was the first to follow the footsteps of the martyrdom of the Lord." With understandable anachronism Irenaeus returns to this theme: "Luke also has recorded that Stephen, who was the first elected into the assembly by the apostles, and who was the first slain for the testimony of Christ . . ." (Against Heresies, 3: 12, 10; 4: 15, 1).[2]

In Northern Africa, when Christianity flourished in that part of the third world, Tertullian wrote of deacons and of women who performed diaconal functions. The rigoristic Tertullian gave momentum to dualistic thought currents then flowing against remarriage by church ministers, including the order of widows.

> The law of the Church and the precept of the apostle show clearly how prejudicial second marriages are to the faith and how great an obstacle to holiness. For men who have been married twice are not allowed to preside in the church. Nor is it permissible that a widow be chosen unless she is the wife of but one man (To His Wife, 7).[3]

Widows were "chosen" and not ordained. Many early Chris-

2. Irenaeus of Lyons, "Against Heresies," in *The Writings of Irenaeus*, Alexander Roberts, ed., Edinburgh, 1880, pp. 307-308, 419.

3. Tertullian, "To His Wife," *Treatises on Marriage and Remarriage*, William Le Saint, ed., (Ancient Christian Writers), Westminster, 1951, p. 20.

tian writers were hardly liberationists. Women also served, but not within the male triadic ministry.

During his Montanist phase Tertullian was horrified to learn that a bishop admitted a nubile twenty year old to the order of widows. This order served by giving advice and solace, and only a mature woman could do that.

> I know very well that they have chosen for the order of widows a virgin hardly twenty years of age. But this order is for women over sixty years of age, not only for those who have been married only once, but for mothers of a family, for those who have raised children, who have experienced the human affections; those know best how to help others with advice and solace, because they have experienced those things which prove the true woman. It is not permitted to honor virgins in this order.[4]

In Tertullian's treatise on monogamy we learn that deacons, as well as bishops and presbyters, were to be men of one marriage. We also observe that deacons and widows assisted at the marriage liturgy.

> How will you dare request the kind of marriage which is not permitted to the ministers from whom you ask it, the bishop who is a monogamist, the presbyters and deacons who are bound by the same solemn obligation, the widows whose way of life you repudiate in your own person (Monogamy, 11).[5]

---

4. PL, 2, 951.

5. Tertullian, "Monogamy," *Treatises on Marriage and Remarriage,* p. 93.

Needless to say not all ministers were as enthusiastic about monogamy as Tertullian implied. Like their successors in the secular age ministers were plainly convinced that it was better to remarry than to burn. While Tertullian was extolling the abstinence of widowed ministers, Hippolytus complained at Rome about bishops, priests and deacons "who have been twice married and thrice married" and who, with the help and consolation of a woman they loved were "allowed to take their place among the clergy." [6] In our own day when it is fashionable to observe that human nature is evolving, it is worth noting the similarities between Tertullian and Hippolytus' horror of remarried ministers and the attitude of today's Catholic bishops to a married clergy. No less interesting is the parallel response of second century clergy and today's clergy to these attitudes.

In Tertullian's Africa deacons baptized — but only with a commission from their bishop. Early sacralization of the Christian ministry is apparent in Tertullian's view of the bishop as "high priest" and the laity as "even laymen." Yet Tertullian correctly saw the necessity of union with the bishop and the ancillary role of deacons and presbyters.

It remains for me to advise you of the rules to be observed in giving and receiving baptism. The supreme right of giving it belongs to the high priest, which is the bishop; after him to the presbyters and deacons, yet not without commission from the bishop, on account of the church's dignity: for

---

6. Hippolytus, "The Refutation of All Heresies," in *The Ante-Nicene Fathers*, Alexander Roberts and James Donaldson, eds., Vol. 5, Edinburgh, 1919, p. 131.

when this is safe, peace is safe. Except for that, even laymen have the right (On Baptism, 17).[7]

Baptism was a service that deacons, but not widows, could give. Tertullian saw no role for women in baptizing or preaching: "How should we believe that Paul would give a female power to teach and to baptize, when he did not allow a woman to learn by her own right. 'Let them keep silence,' he says, 'and ask their husbands at home' " (Ibid.).

The role of deacons differed not only from widows but also from presbyters. According to Eusebius, Pope Cornelius lamented the refusal of the presbyter Novation to minister to God's people. Deacons begged Novation to leave his seclusion and perform his ministry, but Novation refused to give the services a presbyter could give.

. . . he who through cowardice and love of living in the time of persecution denied that he was a presbyter. For, when he was asked and entreated by the deacons to come out of the chamber in which he had enclosed himself, and give aid to his brethren as is right and possible for a presbyter to aid brethren who are in danger and need assistance, far from obeying the exhortations of the deacons he departed and left even in anger. He said that he did not wish to be a presbyter, since he was enamored of another philosophy (Eccl. Hist. 6:43).[8]

---

7. *Tertullian's Homily on Baptism*, Ernest Evans, ed., London, 1964, pp. 35-36.

8. Eusebius Pamphili, *Ecclesiastical History*, (*Books 6-10*), Roy Defferrari, ed., (The Fathers of the Church), N. Y. 1953, p. 84.

In the middle of the third century, from 248 to 258, Cyprian served as bishop of Carthage. His episcopacy was beset by turmoil. Cyprian's pastoral writings for a Church suffering from persecution provide invaluable information about the diaconal function in the third century. In his treatise on "lapsed" Christians who had accommodated themselves to persecutors, Cyprian describes the embarrassment of a young girl who was reluctant to receive communion. His moving description reveals that in Africa deacons distributed the cup to communicants.

> When, however, the solemnities were finished and the deacon began to offer the cup to those present, and when, as the rest received it, its turn approached, the little child by the instinct of the divine majesty, turned away its face, compressed its mouth with resisting lips and refused the cup. Still the deacon persisted and, although against her efforts, forced on her some of the sacrament of the cup (On the Lapsed, 25).[9]

During the Decian persecution Cyprian guided his people by pastoral letters from his hiding place. Under these unusual conditions it is understandable that some deacons went astray. He complained about errant deacons and presbyters. His remarks indicate that deacons served at the eucharistic liturgy.

---

9. Cyprian, "On the Lapsed," in *The Ante-Nicene Fathers,* Alexander Roberts and James Donaldson, eds., Vol. 5, Edinburgh, 1919, p. 444. All references to Cyprian's writings are taken from this volume.

Cyprian to the presbyters and deacons, his brethren, greetings. You have done uprightly and with discipline, beloved
brethren, that, by the advice of my colleagues who were
present, you decided not to communicate with Gaius the
presbyter and his deacon; who, by communicating with the
lapsed and offering their oblations have been frequently
taken in by their errors (Ep. 27:1).

Deacons and "priests" who worshipped with heretics and
"attempted to offer, in opposition to the one divine altar, false
and sacrilegious sacrifices," were to be received back into
communion only as laymen. "For it becomes priests and ministers who wait upon the altar and sacrifices to be sound and
stainless" (Ep. 51:2).

Cyprian delegated presbyters and deacons to administer
his church or "diocese" while he was hindered by persecution.
The African church experience is instructive for our own time
of turmoil and dehumanizing urbanization. The role of presbyters and deacons were extended to meet the extraordinary
needs of the particular time and place in which they served.

Cyprian to the presbyters and deacons, his beloved brethren, greetings. Being by the grace of God in safety, dearest
brethren, I salute you, rejoicing that I am informed of the
prosperity of all things in respect of the prosperity of your
safety; and as the condition of the place does not permit
me to be with you now, I beg you, by your faith and your
religion, to discharge there both your own office and mine,
that there may be nothing wanting either to discipline or
diligence (Ep. 4:1).

With Cyprian in hiding and unable to visit his people deacons accompanied presbyters in visitations. This ministry almost certainly included assistance at the Eucharist. "The presbyters also, who there offer with the confessors, may one by one take turns with the deacons individually." But at least one deacon remained at Cyprian's side. "Victor the deacon, and all those who are with me, greet you" (*Ibid.*).

Cyprian argued that the apostles appointed deacons as ministers of the episcopacy and the church. He exhorted a recalcitrant deacon to cooperate with his bishop.

> Deacons ought to remember that the Lord chose apostles, that is bishops and overseers; while apostles appointed for themselves deacons after the ascent of the Lord into heaven, as ministers of their episcopacy of the church. But if we may dare anything against God who makes bishops, deacons may also dare against us by whom they are made and therefore it behooves the deacon of whom you write . to repent of his audacity, and to acknowledge the honor of the priest and to satisfy the bishop set over him with full humility (Ep. 54:3).

Yet deacons and presbyters shared responsibility with the bishop in government of the church. From the enforced isolation of his hiding place Cyprian expressed the wish that the entire hierarchy "might be able to consult together on those matters which are required by the general advantage, in respect of the government of the church, and having carefully examined them with abundant counsel, might wisely arrange them" (Ep. 4:1).

The bishop depended on presbyters and deacons for information so that he could advise them how to administer the church. Deacons, therefore, were mediators of information concerning the needs of the community. Cyprian complained about ministers who were negligent in this service.

> I marvel, beloved brethren, that you have answered nothing to me in reply to my many letters which I have frequently written to you, although as well the advantage as the need of our brotherhood would certainly be best provided for if, receiving information from you, I could accurately investigate and advise upon the management of affairs (Ep. 12:1).

During the persecution deacons were on occasion ordinary ministers of confession and reconciliation. Although distinctions of internal and external forum had yet to develop, there is definite precedent in Cyprian's Africa for deacons hearing confessions.

> They who have received certificates from the martyrs, and may be assisted by their privilege with God, if they should be seized with any misfortune and peril of sickness, should, without waiting for my presence, before any presbyter who might be present, or if a presbyter should not be found and death becomes imminent, before even a deacon, be able to make confession of their sins, that, with the imposition of hands upon them for repentance, they should come to the Lord with the peace which the martyrs have desired, by their letter to us, be granted to them (Ep. 12:1).

In a subsequent letter Cyprian reminded presbyters and deacons of their commission to hear confessions and impose hands on *certificati* in grave need.

> I think I have sufficiently written on this subject in the last letter that was sent to you, that they who have received a certificate from the martyrs, and can be assisted by their help with the Lord in respect of their sins, if they begin to be oppressed with any sickness or risk; when they have made confession, and have received the imposition of hands on them by you in acknowledgment of their penitence, should be remitted to the Lord with that peace promised to them by the martyrs (Ep. 13:2).

We may conclude that the diaconal function was adapted to contemporary needs of liturgy, word, and charity. Reconciling penitents includes all three. The great Cyprian did not feel constrained in his use of deacons by the functions deacons had performed in other ages with other needs.

But Cyprian followed Irenaeus in regarding the seven Jerusalem hellenists as permanent deacons. Despite this anachronism he drives home an important requirement for authentic ministry. There is no such thing as a "free" ministry if the person who claims to be a minister is not recognized by the community as their minister. The apostles called together "the *whole* of the people" that no unworthy person might function in the ministry.

> Neither do we observe that this was regarded by the apostles only in the ordinations of bishops and priests, but also in

those of deacons, of which matter itself also it is written in Acts: 'And the twelve called together,' it says, 'the whole congregation of the disciples, and said to them'; which was done so diligently and carefully, together with the calling together of the whole of the people, slowly for this reason, that no unworthy person might creep into the ministry of the altar, or to the office of a priest (Ep. 57:4).

We also observe in Cyprian two familiar themes in the history of the diaconate: 1) deacons were official ministers of the church's charity; and 2) some deacons betrayed this trust by stealing money destined for the poor. The concern of Paul, Hermas, and Polycarp that deacons be honest men was well founded.

Nicostratus, having lost the diaconate of sacred administrations, because he had abstracted the church's money by a sacrilegious fraud, and disowned the deposits of the widows and orphans, did not wish so much to come into Africa as to escape thither from the city, from the consciousness of his rapines and frightful crimes (Ep. 58:1).

In Cyprian's Africa as in the Rome of Hippolytus "clerics" in minor orders appear. Sub-deacons served as letter bearers (Ep. 29:1; 40:1). There were exorcists, readers (Ep. 29:1) and acolytes (Ep. 27). Cyprian spoke of a "clergy" which included even the reader Celerinus who was "ordained" to the "clergy." "Exult, therefore, and rejoice with me on receiving my letters, wherein I and my colleagues who were then present mention to you Celerinus, our brother, glorious alike for his courage and his character, as added to our clergy" (Ep. 33:1).

There was an order of virgins in Africa, but Cyprian's views on marriage and sex reflect Tertullian's influence. The virgins, because they lived as eunuchs, were destined for the better habitations among the heavenly mansions.

> Now when the world is filled and the earth supplied, they who can receive continency, living after the manner of eunuchs, are made eunuchs unto the kingdom. Nor does the Lord command this; but he exhorts it; nor does he impose the yoke of necessity, since the free choice of the will is left. But when he says that in his Father's house are many mansions, he points out the dwellings of the better habitation. Those better habitations you are seeking; cutting away the desires of the flesh, you obtain the reward of a greater grace in the heavenly home (On the Dress of Virgins, 23).

In plain proof that there is nothing new under the sun, Cyprian responded to an anxious query about a pre-Nicene "third way." It seems that some sworn virgins were sleeping with men without having intercourse with them. Cyprian was less than enthusiastic about this venture in brinksmanship. As coincidence would have it, one of the young men who engaged in this experiment was an adventuresome deacon.

> We have read, dearest brother, your letter which you sent by Paconius, our brother, asking and desiring us to write again to you, and say what we thought of those virgins who, after having once determined to continue in their condition, and firmly to maintain their continency,

have afterwards been found to have remained in the same bed side by side with men; of whom you say that one is a deacon; . . . you have acted advisedly and with vigor, dearest brother, in excommunicating the deacon who has often abode with a virgin; and moreover, the others who had been used to sleep with virgins (Ep. 41:1, 4).

As a rule, however, deacons were loyal associates of their bishop. When Cyprian was martyred at Carthage, September 14, 258, his deacons stepped forward to stand beside him. That same year the Bishop of Rome was arrested with four of his deacons as they were officiating in the catacombs. They died together on August 6. Four days later the principal deacon of that city, Laurentius, followed his colleagues. Lawrence had distributed the church's wealth to the poor during the Valerian persecution. As the much loved St. Lawrence he became a famous martyr saint of the Roman Church.

In third century Egypt, as in Africa, there was a clearly structured ministry of bishop, presbyters, and deacons. For Clement of Alexandria the hierarchical "grades" on earth reflected the heavenly economy. "According to my opinion the grades here in the church of bishop, presbyters, deacons are imitators of the angelic glory of the heavenly economy which, the scriptures say, awaits those who, following the footsteps of the apostles, have lived in perfection of righteousness according to the gospel" (Strom. 6: 13).[10] For Origen ministry of the word was of paramount importance. He compares dea-

---

10. Clement of Alexandria, *Stromata*, in *The Ante-Nicene Fathers*, Vol. 2, A. Cleveland Coxe, ed., N. Y., 1925, p. 505.

cons to levites who minister the word of God. "When you see priests and levites no longer handling the blood of rams and bulls, but ministering the word of God by the grace of the Holy Spirit, then you can say that Jesus has taken the place of Moses" (Homilies on Joshua, 2:6).[11]

According to Eusebius, Denis of Alexandria reported that presbyters, deacons and laity gave their lives in ministration to the sick during war and persecution. "The best, at any rate, of the brethren among us departed from life in this manner, some presbyters, and deacons, and some of the laity who were praised exceedingly, so that this form of death, which had its origin in much piety and strong faith, seemed to be little short of martyrdom" (Eccl. Hist. 7:22).

At Rome Pope Fabian (235-250) divided the eternal city into seven administrative districts, each under the authority of a deacon.[12] According to Eusebius there were at Rome "forty six presbyters, seven deacons, seven sub-deacons, forty two acolytes, fifty two exorcists, readers together with doorkeepers, more than fifteen hundred widows with persons in distress, all of whom the grace and kindness of the Master supported" (Eccl. Hist. 6: 43).

An important document that provides invaluable information about the pre-Nicene diaconate is *The Apostolic Tradition* of Hippolytus. This early church order, written about 215, is a conservative document which purports to preserve apostolic rite and polity. It illuminates the diaconal function dating back into the second century. The *Tradition* also

---

11. PG, 12, 833.
12. Walter Croce, "Histoire du Diaconat," in *Le Diacre Dans L'Eglise,* pp. 37-38.

provides information about the subsequent diaconate, for it was translated into Latin, Syriac, Ethiopic, Arabic, Sahidic, and Bohairic.

Hippolytus recognized the importance of deacons, but he wished to restrain them. The man he opposed above all others was the former archdeacon who became Pope Callistus. Significantly, archdeacons assisted the bishop in administration of the cemetery and *management of the clergy.* Hippolytus, the presbyter, thought this exceeded the deacon's role. Although the only power he explicitly committed to presbyters and forbade to deacons was the imposition of hands at the ordination of a presbyter, Hippolytus tried to make clear that presbyters with the bishop were the governing body in the Church.

In the ordination of *deacons,* only the bishop and *not the presbyters* imposed hands. But this rite was not meant to exalt deacons nor humble presbyters; on the contrary, it placed the diaconate in proper proportion or, in modern parlance, it put deacons in their place.

And a deacon when he is appointed shall be chosen according to what has been said before, the bishop alone laying hands on him in the same manner . . . The bishop alone shall lay hands at the ordination of a deacon for this reason: that he is not ordained for a priesthood, but for the service of the bishop that he may do the things commanded by him. For he is not the fellow counsellor of the whole clergy but to take charge of property and to report to the bishop whatever is necessary. He does not receive the Spirit which is common to all the presbyterate, in which the presbyters share, but that which is entrusted to him under the bishop's authority. Nor is he appointed to receive the spirit of greatness which presbyters share (The Apostolic Tradition, 9).[13]

But deacons were clearly superior to sub-deacons. At Rome where deacons administered the seven districts, "Hands shall not be laid on a sub-deacon but he shall be named that he may serve the deacon" (74).

Nor were Roman widows ordained; they were "appointed" and "chosen." "When a widow is appointed she is not ordained but she shall be chosen by name." Only males were ordained for liturgical ministry. "Let the widow be instituted by name only and then let her be reckoned among the enrolled widows. But she shall not be ordained, because she does not offer the oblation nor does she a liturgical ministry." The development of important roles for women in the church, so promisingly begun in the first letter to Timothy was opposed by writers such as Tertullian, Cyprian, and Hippolytus. "But ordination is for the clergy on account of their liturgical ministry. But the widow is appointed for prayer and this is a function of all Christians" (71). Virgins were not even appointed, but "separated and named." "The virgin is not appointed but separated and named. A virgin does not have imposition of hands, for personal choice alone is that which makes a virgin" (13).

The Apostolic Tradition and its many versions which spread across the Christian world exceeded Paul's original reluctance

---

13. In quotations from the Apostolic Tradition I am following rather loosely the reconstruction of Gregory Dix in The Apostolic Tradition of Hippolytus, Gregory Dix, ed., London, 1937.

to admit women to ministry of the word and leadership. The author of Timothy did not permit women to teach; Tertullian forbade women to baptize; Cyprian and Hippolytus tolerated merely the prayer of widows and the mute witness of virgins. Henceforth the diaconal function, in those regions most influenced by Tertullian and Hippolytus, would devolve almost exclusively on male deacons. In Syria widows and deaconesses would continue to perform vital services. But ultimately the encratism of North Africa and Rome would prevail. A hundred years after Hippolytus, the great Council of Nicea would state clearly that deaconesses were not to receive imposition of hands because they were in fact numbered "among the laity."

But for male deacons the third century, despite gathering storms, was a golden age. Deacons brought forth the sacred oblations at the consecration of a bishop: "To him then let all the deacons bring the oblations." Their function was also important at the Paschal Mass: "And then let the oblations at once be brought by the deacon to the bishop . . ." (23). If there were insufficient presbyters, "the deacon also — shall hold the cup and stand by in good order . . ." (*Ibid*). In the Ethiopic version deacons broke bread at the Stational Mass: "On the first day of the week the bishop, if it is possible, shall with his own hand deliver to all the people, while the deacons break the bread" (24).

Deacons were prominent at the Roman baptismal liturgy. "Let a deacon carry the Oil of Exorcism and stand on the left hand of the presbyter who will do the anointing. And another deacon shall take the Oil of Thanksgiving and stand on the right hand" (27).

But some deacons were careless about attendance at chapter. Hippolytus admonished them to be faithful every day. "And let the deacons and presbyters assemble daily at the place which the bishop shall appoint for them. And let not the deacons especially neglect to assemble every day unless sickness prevents them" (33).

In the absence of a bishop or presbyter, deacons presided at *agape*. "And if the faithful shall be present at a supper without the bishop but with a presbyter or deacon present, let them similarly partake in orderly fashion. But let everyone be careful to receive the blessed bread at the hand of a presbyter or deacon" (26).

The deacon was a special minister to the needs of the sick. "And let each of the deacons with the sub-deacons attend upon the bishop; and let it be reported to him who are sick, that if it seems good to the bishop he may visit them; for the sick man is much comforted that the high priest remembered him" (30).

At the source of the mighty Nile deacons may have enjoyed the power of anointing. In the Ethiopic version "The deacon in time of need shall be diligent in giving the sealing to the sick." Even if this important sentence is a later interpolation it may be significant in the history of the diaconate. For at some times and places deacons may have been official ministers of anointing.[14] However, the *Testament of our Lord*, which is less favorable to deacons than is the Ethiopic version of the *Tradition* interprets Hippolytus as allowing deacons, in the absence of a presbyter, to *baptize* the sick. "Let the deacon,

---

14. Gregory Dix, himself a sacerdotalist, admits that the Ethiopic Version of the *Tradition* "perhaps has in mind unction," *Ibid.*, p. 49, note 14.

when the presbyter is not present, of necessity baptize" (26).

An important third century document which is more favorable to deacons than the Greek *Apostolic Tradition* and the later *Testament of Our Lord,* is the Syrian *Didascalia Apostolorum.* The author of this pastoral order, stressing the importance of bishop and deacons, relegates presbyters to a surprisingly modest role. In Syria of the *Didascalia* women too performed more important diaconal functions than in the Latin West.

The author, probably a bishop, is influenced by the letters of Ignatius; he compares the bishop to God, the presbyters to the apostles, and the deacons to Christ. Deaconesses are compared to the Spirit, for in Hebrew and Aramaic "spirit" is feminine. "The bishop sits in the place of God Almighty. But the deacon stands in the place of Christ; and do you love him. And the deaconess shall be honored by you in the place of the Holy Spirit, and the presbyter shall be to you in the likeness of the apostles" (Didasc. 9).[15]

Deacons are compared to Christ for two reasons. First, their service is that of Christ the *diaconos* washing his disciples' feet; second, their service is that of Christ the mediator reporting men's needs to the Father.

> If then our Lord did thus, will you, O deacons, hesitate to do the like for them that are sick and infirm, you who are workmen of the truth, and bear the likeness of Christ? ... It is required of you deacons, therefore, that you visit all who are in need, and inform the bishop of those who

---

15. *Didascalia Apostolorum,* R. H. Connolly, ed., Oxford, 1929. In quotations from the *Didascalia* I am following strictly Dom Connolly's translation of the Syriac version.

are in need, and inform the bishop of those who are in distress; and you shall be his soul and mind; and in all things you shall be taking trouble and be obedient to him (26).

Three other recurrent themes appear. First, deacons are admonished not to be greedy; second, there are to be sufficient deacons for the size of the congregation; third, deacons are special ministers of the sick and aged.

And let them not love filthy lucre; but let them be diligent in the ministry. And in proportion to the minister of the congregation of the people of the church, so let the deacons be, that they may be able to take knowledge (of each) severally and replenish all; so that for the aged women who are infirm, and for brethren and sisters who are in sickness — for every one they may provide the ministry which is proper for him (16).

Deacons therefore were servants of those in distress. "And let the deacon go in to those who are in distress and let them visit each one and provide him with what he lacks" (18).

Deacons were supported by the congregation. In fact they deserved the same support as presbyters and more than the widows. "But how much silver is given to one of the widows, let the double be given to each of the deacons in honor of Christ, (but) twice two-fold to the leader for the glory of the Almighty. But if any one wish to honor the presbyters also, let him give them a double (portion) as to the deacons." The laity were to make known their needs to the bishop through the mediation of deacons who, as we have seen, were compared to Christ the mediator. "But let them have free access to the deacons, and let them not be troubling the head at all times, but making known what they require through the ministers, that is through the deacons. For neither can any man approach the Lord God Almighty except through Christ" (9).

The author of the *Didascalia,* in claiming apostolic authorship for his treatise, attests to his own presence at the Council of Jerusalem. The importance of deacons to the episcopalist author comes through when he reports the presence of "deacons" at the Jerusalem Council. ". . . and not we the apostles only, but also the people, together with James the bishop of Jerusalem, who is our Lord's brother after the flesh, and with his presbyters and deacons and all the church" (24). Repeatedly the close union, even identity between deacon and bishop is stressed by the author. "But for us, now, Aaron is the deacon, and Moses is the bishop. Now if Moses was called a god by the Lord, let the bishop also be honored by you as God, and the deacon as a prophet" (9). "For what hope at all is there for him who speaks evil of the bishop, or of the deacon? . . . If then one who should say any of these things to a layman is found to fall under so great a condemnation, how much more if he should dare to say ought against the deacon, or against the bishop . . ." (*Ibid.*).

The deacon was of one mind, purpose and soul with the bishop.

And let him be ready to obey and to submit himself to the command of the bishop. And let him labor and toil in every place whither he is sent to minister or to speak of some matter to any one. For it behooves each one to know his office and be diligent in executing it. And be you (bishop and deacon) of one council and of one purpose, and one soul dwelling in two bodies (16).

The *Didascalia's* prescriptions for worship reiterate the now venerable tradition that deacons performed important but subordinate roles at the Eucharist. They were assistants to the bishop who presided at the east end of the building flanked by his council of presbyters.

But of the deacons let one stand always by the oblations of the Eucharist; and let another stand without by the door and observe them that come in; and afterwards, when you offer let them minister together in the Church. And if any one be found sitting out of his place, let the deacon who is within reprove him and make him to rise up and sit in a place that is meet for him ... And let the deacon see that each of them on entering goes to his place, that no one may sit out of his place. And let the deacon also see that no one whispers, or falls asleep, or laughs, or makes signs.

When visitors from neighboring communities approached for worship, the deacon escorted them to their proper place. Presbyters welcomed visiting presbyters; if a bishop presented himself, the presiding bishop invited him to address the congregation. The ordinary role of the deacon at the Eucharist was a humble one. "But if, while younger men or women sit, an older man or woman should rise and give up their place, do thou, O deacon, scan those who sit, to see which man or woman of them is younger than the rest, and make them stand up, and cause him to sit who had risen and given up his place" (92).

The *Didascalia* reveals the role of deacons in reconciling Christians. When reconciliation was communal, permanent deacons invited the people to reconciliation.

> Wherefore, O bishops, that your oblations and your prayers may be acceptable, when you stand in the church to pray let the deacon say with a loud voice: 'Is there any man that keepeth ought against his fellow?' that if there be found any who have a lawsuit or quarrel one with another, thou mayest entreat them and make peace between them (11).

We may conclude from the *Didascalia* that the deacon's role at the Eucharist and in penitential preparations was an important but ancillary one. There is no evidence in the *Didascalia* that deacons presided at the Eucharist or heard confessions. But this argument is from silence and should not be pressed. Earlier and later evidence indicates that on occasion deacons performed central functions in the liturgy.

In Syria an active order of widows collaborated with deacons and deaconesses. Woman's role in the east therefore, was diminished but not suppressed by the influence of writers such as Tertullian, Hippolytus and Cyprian. The age limit for appointment to the order of widows was lowered to fifty in Syria instead of the traditional sixty. But widows were not to remarry. "Appoint as a widow one that is not under fifty years old, who in some sort, by reason of her years, shall be remote from the suspicion of taking a second husband." Widows prayed for the community.

> And when she is asked a question by any one; let her not straightway give an answer, except only concerning righteousness and faith in God; but let her send them that desire to be instructed to the rulers . . . . It is neither right nor necessary that women should be teachers, and especially concerning the name of Christ and the redemption of His passion. For you have not been appointed to this, O women, and especially widows, that you should teach, but that you should pray and entreat the Lord God (11).

Yet even the widows in Tertullian's Africa were appointed to *pray*. In the Syria of the *Didascalia* they did considerably more. They obeyed the bishop and deacons; but when these officers so commanded, widows were commissioned to lay hands upon the sick.

> Widows ought then to be modest, and obedient to the bishops and deacons, and to reverence and respect and fear the bishop as God. And let them not act after their own wile, nor desire to do anything apart from that which is commanded them, or without counsel to speak with anyone by way of making answer, or to go to any one to eat or drink, or to fast with anyone, or to receive ought of anyone, or to lay hand on and pray over any one without the command of the bishop or deacon (15).

Deaconesses were appointed to collaborate with deacons, especially in ministration to women: "Those that please thee out of all the people thou shalt choose and appoint as deacons; a man for the performance of the most things that are required, but a woman for the ministry of women." Examples of this ministry for women were visitation, anointing of the body at baptism, and rudimentary instruction. It is noteworthy that even when women were baptized, a deaconess was not permitted to announce the invocation.

> ". . . whether thou (bishop) thyself baptize, or thou commission the presbyters or deacons to baptize — let a woman deacon, as we have already said, anoint the women. But let a man announce over them the invocation of the divine name in the water."

The author, like his predecessors, draws back from admitting women to a complete share in the diaconate. Their share was vitally important; but it was incomplete.

> And when she who is being baptized has come up from the water, let the deaconess secure her, and teach and instruct her how the seal of baptism ought to be (kept) unbroken in purity and holiness. For this cause we say that the ministry of a woman deacon is especially needful and important. For our Lord and Savior also was ministered unto by women ministers, Mary Magdalene, and Mary the daughter of James and mother of Jose, and the mother of the sons of Zebedee, with other women beside (16).

There are already in the *Apostolic Tradition* and the *Didascalia* indications of tension between bishops and deacons on the one hand and presbyters on the other. Hippolytus was concerned to keep deacons in their place; the *Didascalia* exalts them. This tension continues to develop in the fourth century.

Another tension is manifested in the restrictive legislation of early synodal documents on clerical celibacy. Already at Elvira (c. 305) bishops, presbyters, and deacons were ordered to forego conjugal relations or "be removed from the honor of the clerical state." [16] Needless to say these seminal episcopal ventures in dualism were heeded more in the breach than in the observance. But the seeds of the celibacy problem were planted.

In 314 the Council of Arles says that deacons are offering [17] (*offerre*) "in many places." In synodal documents of the time *offerre* meant presidency at the Eucharist, a function which Arles forbids deacons to exercise. Three points call for remark: 1) Arles does not say that a Eucharist offered by deacons is "invalid" nor that deacons lack all power to confect the Eucharist. The fathers simply state that deacons had offered in many places and that the practice should cease; 2) the decree by its prohibition indicates that in many places congregations had recognized deacons as authentic presidents at

---

16. *Sacrorum Consiliorum Nova et Amplissima Collectio,* J. D. Mansi, ed., Leipzig, 1901, Vol. 1, p. 11.

17. *Ibid.,* Vol. 2, p. 474. The Latin of the prohibition of deacons "offering" reads as follows: *De diaconibus quos cognovimus multis locis offerre placuit minime fieri debere.* The Council of Nicea in Canon 18 refers to presbyters as those who *offerre* the Eucharist and deacons as those who do not.

the Eucharist; 3) another council, held in Ancyra (314), concerned itself with deacons who "immolate," who "offer," and who "pronounce." [18] This may refer to functions ancillary to the president, but the probability is that early in the fourth century deacons occasionally presided at the Eucharist until this ministry was forbidden by synodal decree.

The legislation of the Constantinian epoch demonstrates that the ministry of deacons was an accepted part of Church order. Some synodal canons legislated for deacons along with bishops and presbyters; others concern themselves solely with deacons. In retrospect we know that permanent deacons were not there to stay; but they were there.

Arles, for example, ordered deacons to assist and not supplant presbyters.[19] But deacons sat at Arles itself and signed for absent bishops. Ancyra, in a remarkable canon, dealt with deacons who married *after* ordination. If before their ordination deacons informed the bishop of their intention to marry they were permitted to take wives even *after* ordination. If before ordination they were silent about their nuptial intentions they must, if they marry, "cease from the diaconate." [20] Laodicea (c. 345) permits deacons to sit only at the command of a presbyter, while subdeacons and lesser clerics are to show similar deference to deacons. Unlike the "lesser" clergy deacons entered the sacristy, handled the vessels, and wore the stole or *orarion*. Deacons also presided at the community *agape*.[21]

---

18. *Ibid.*, pp. 514, 523.
19. *Ibid.*, pp. 474, 475.
20. *Ibid.*, p. 518.
21. *Ibid.*, pp. 567, 579, 587.

There were five deacons at an early Council at Rome.[22] Neo-Caesarea (c. 320) referring to the seven hellenists, reduces the number of deacons to seven.[23] Athanasius, while still a deacon, took an active part in the deliberations at Nicea (325).

Nicea legislated for all the clergy.[24] Although eastern bishops dominated the assembly, presbyters were given unequivocal precedence over deacons whose privileges were curtailed. Where deaconesses were concerned the fathers were anything but feminist. Deaconesses, the Council made clear, "were numbered among the laity" (canon 19). Celibacy was well on its way to centuries of semi-observance and conflict. Clerics were forbidden to consort with women except for close relatives and other persons, free of suspicion. The bishops present at Nicea made no exceptions for themselves, but chose to burn with lesser clerics.

> This great synod forbids altogether that it should be allowed to a bishop or presbyter or deacon, or to anyone in the clergy, to have a woman *introductam* unless she be mother or sister or relative, or those persons alone, who give no suspicion (Canon 3).[24]

Attempting to stem the tide of migrant clerics the Council forbade bishops, presbyters and deacons to wander from region to region. Presbyters and deacons who present themselves to other churches are not to be admitted; rather, they are to be

---

22. *Ibid.,* p. 670.
23. *Ibid.,* p. 546.
24. *Ibid.,* pp. 670f.

told to return to their own communities. If they persist they are to be "separated from communion." If they still persevere in their audacity their ordination is made void (*irrita*) (Canon 16).

Canon 18 concerned itself solely with deacons, reaffirming their historic role as assistants to the bishop. At the Eucharist they assisted the bishop and presbyters. They were "less" than presbyters and if they were discontented with their grade they should cease from the diaconate. Nicea took permanent deacons for granted, but it hardly exalted them.

It has come to the attention of the synod that in some regions deacons give the eucharist to presbyters. This is in accord neither with canon nor custom, that those who do not have the power of offering give the body of Christ to those who offer. Moreover, it is also known that some deacons attain the eucharist before the bishop. Let those things cease and let deacons remain within their proper place, knowing that they are ministers of the bishop and less than presbyters. Let them receive the Eucharist in their proper order after presbyters, distributed to them by the bishop or a presbyter. Nor may a deacon sit in the midst of the presbyters. This is done contrary to canon and order. If anyone does not wish to obey after these constitutions, let him desist from the diaconate (Canon 18).

Conclusion

In the era from Ignatius to Nicea the permanent deacon enjoyed the *apogee* of his golden age. He was taken for granted

by people and council alike. But with the developing sacralization of presbyters, the seeds of his decline were planted. It
is a luxury to be taken for granted, and in the centuries after
Nicea the permanent deacon was to see this luxury decline and
vanish.

Nicea to the Reformation: Decline of the Diaconate

During the long and eventful centuries from Nicea to the reformation the permanent diaconate at first flourished and then declined. The seeds of diaconal decline were already planted with the rise of sacerdotalism in the third century and the restrictive legislation of the early fourth century. A confusion of roles between deacons and "priests" and a struggle for identity continued into the Middle Ages. Gradually the diaconate receded in importance until the diaconal order became merely a preliminary and ceremonial step to the sacralized priesthood.

But in the fourth and fifth centuries deacons continued to perform important services in the Church. The *Apostolic Constitutions,* a fourth century Church order compiled at Syria or Constantinople, illustrates that in the post-Nicene era deacons were still important church officers. According to the *Constitutions* deacons represented their bishop at synods when the latter was unable to attend and presided with other ministers over solemn assemblies when quarrels among Christians were adjudicated (2:47, 1).[1]

Deacons merely assisted at baptism; they did not baptize (5:11,1). At the Eucharist they read the gospel and announced the prayers of the faithful (8:13, 2); they assigned worshippers

---

1. *Didascalia et Constitutiones Apostolorum,* F. X. Funk, ed., Paderborn, 1905, p. 143.

their proper place in the new Christian churches, guarded order and decorum, and prevented interruptions by outsiders. During the anaphora they stood at the bishop's side (2:57, 6).

The *Constitutions* reiterated the relatively liberal legislation of Ancyra (314-319) and several other synods about the marriage of deacons. If before ordination they declared their marital intentions they were permitted to take a wife; otherwise, upon marriage they ceased to be deacons (6:17, 1). Deacons, no less than bishop and presbyters, were supported by the congregation (2:28, 3).

Deaconesses were usually considered subordinate to deacons. At the Eucharist, for example, they received only one piece of bread while the deacon received two (8:30). Deaconesses communicated the needs and desires of women to the presiding bishop (2:26), guarded the door through which women entered the church, and escorted women worshippers to their proper place (2:57).

Deaconesses were received into the ministry through a ceremony which was surprisingly similar to the ordination of male clerics. The bishop imposed hands on the candidate in the presence of deaconesses, deacons, and presbyters. Moreover, there was a solemn invocation "on this your servant, chosen for the ministry, and give to her your Holy Spirit, and cleanse her from every stain of flesh and spirit, that she may worthily do the work committed to her" (8:19). This solemnity of ordering of women, which is mentioned again in the documents of Chalcedon (451) and Trullo (692), was apparently limited to the East.

The *Apostolic Constitutions* include eighty-five canons which summarize much of the legislation of early fourth century synods. There is a surprising amount of legislation concerning deacons. This indicates: 1) that deacons were still prominent in the East and, 2) they were gradually and with some difficulty being brought under juridical control.

Deacons were forbidden to offer the eucharist (8:46). Only one bishop was to ordain a deacon (8:2). Bishops who received vagrant deacons were to be punished (8:15-16). Traveling deacons were to be received only when they presented an authentic letter of recommendation (8:33). Deacons could take a wife, but could not marry an actress, widow, slave, nor public woman (8:18). Deacons were supported by the community; they assisted the bishop in services of charity to the indigent (8:4).

Deacons were degraded for seeking reordination from a second bishop (8:68), for leaving their diocese (8:15), for refusing to minister (8:36), for not behaving as clerics (8:84), for injuring a bishop (8:55), for insulting a ruler (8:84), for cooperating with a degraded cleric (8:11), for permitting heretics to perform sacred ministries (8:45), for serving in the army (8:83), for engaging in mundane affairs (8:6), for fornication, perjury, or theft (8:25), for leaving a wife on pretext of piety (8:25), for abstaining from marriage, food, or drink for unworthy reasons (8:51), for not fasting when it was prescribed (8:69), for participating in prayer with Jews (8:70), for celebrating the Pasch before Spring Equinox (8:63), and for excusing delinquent faithful or unjust infidels (8:27).

Deacons were excommunicated for refusing to explain their failures to communicate (8:8), for functioning when degraded (8:28), for praying with Jews in the synagogue (8:45), for denying the name of Christ (8:62), and for injuring a cleric or disabled person (8:56). Only the excommunicating bishop could later lift this penalty (8:12).

Meanwhile, Christianity was taking hold in Roman Britain. In 385 a boy named Patrick was born in a Brittonic town to a decuria named Calpurnius who was a married deacon. Patrick's grandfather, Potitus, was a priest. Patrick, the son of a deacon and grandson of a priest, became one of the most successful and best loved missionaries in Christian history.[2]

The great Fathers of the fourth and fifth centuries referred to deacons, but it is clear from their writings that the permanent diaconate was declining. Ambrose of Milan (d. 397) reminded deacons of the sobriety and example expected of their order. "The minister of the Lord should abstain from wine so that he may be upheld by the great witness not only of the faithful, but also of those who are without." As ministers of the altar, deacons were to be virtuous men. "He who sees the minister of the altar adorned with suitable virtues may praise their author, and reverence the Lord who has such servants." [3]

Ambrose's famous contemporary, St. Jerome (d. 419) signalled the decline of the diaconate with his pro-sacerdotal polemics. When he set out to put deacons (and bishops) in proper perspective Jerome had in mind the powerful archdeacons and deacons of the church at Rome. In a letter to "Evangelus" he spelled out a doctrine of the ministry which emphasized

---

2. M. Deanesly, *The Pre-Conquest Church in England*, N.Y., 1961, p. 37.

3. Ambrose of Milan, "On Duties of the Clergy," in *Select Works and Letters*, (A Select Library of Nicene and Post-Nicene Fathers of the Christian Church, Vol. X), N.Y., 1896, p. 41. Hereafter this series will be referred to as NPNF.

the priest's power at the Eucharist. Since presbyters as well as bishops enjoyed this power Jerome saw little difference between them.

I am told that someone has been mad enough to put deacons before presbyters, that is, before bishops. For when the apostle clearly teaches that presbyters are the same as bishops must not a mere server of tables and of widows be insane to set himself up arrogantly over men through whose prayers the body and blood of Christ are made present.[4]

Now were archdeacons a separate order above deacons; they too were merely deacons. "Deacons appoint one of themselves whom they know to be diligent and call him archdeacon" (1).

According to Jerome, deacons were sometimes considered more precious than presbyters. Archdeacons even nominated ordinands for the presbyterate. Jerome reacted to this "abuse" by recalling the reason why the twelve appointed the seven to serve at tables. Presbyters, Jerome argued, were clearly superior to deacons.

But you will say how comes it then that at Rome a presbyter is only ordained on the recommendation of a deacon? To which I reply as follows. Why do you bring forward a custom that exists in one city only? Why do you oppose to the laws of the church a paltry exception which has given rise to arrogance and pride? . . . Their fewness makes

---

4. St. Jerome, "To Evangelus," in *The Principal Works of St. Jerome*, (NPNF), N.Y., 1893, pp. 288-289.

deacons persons of consequence while presbyters are less
thought of owing to their great numbers. But even in the
church of Rome the deacons stand while the presbyters seat
themselves, although bad habits have by degrees so far
crept in that I have seen a deacon, in the absence of a
bishop, seat himself among the presbyters and at social
gatherings give his blessing to them. Those who act thus
must learn that they are wrong and must give heed to the
apostles' words: 'it is not reason that we should leave the
word of God and serve at tables.' They must consider the
reasons which led to the appointment of deacons at the
beginning. They must read the Acts of the Apostles and
bear in mind their true position (2).

In his polemics against a powerful diaconate Jerome re-
vealed that the *permanent* diaconate was already waning. Priests
were true successors of the Jewish sons of Aaron; deacons were
levites of the new dispensation, inferior to priests, and were
"promoted" to the priesthood.

Again when a man is promoted it is from a lower place to
a higher. Either then a presbyter should be ordained a
deacon, from the lesser office, that is, to the more important, to prove that a presbyter is inferior to a deacon;
or if on the other hand it is the deacon that is ordained
presbyter, this latter should recognize that, although he
may be less highly paid than a deacon, he is superior to
him in virtue of his priesthood. In fact as if to tell us
that the traditions handed down by the apostles were taken
by them from the old testament, bishops, presbyters and

deacons occupy in the church the same position as those which were occupied by Aaron, his sons, and the levites in the temple (2).

As in Cyprian's Africa, the deacons in the area of Jerome's Bethlehem occasionally became involved with nubile, albeit vowed, virgins. Jerome castigated Sabinianus, a frustrated cleric, who courted a cloistered virgin by exchanging love letters *via* a cord attached to her window. When dawn broke over the Mediterranean, Sabinianus was accustomed to hasten from tryst to church where he could be observed piously reading the gospels as if he were "a deacon indeed." From the trials of Sabinianus we may derive at least two lessons: 1) in the patristic age, as in our own, celibacy was a gift given to very few, and 2) deacons in the fourth century were ministers of the word.

How careful the lady superior must have been is shown by the fact that you never saw the virgin except in church; and that, although both of you had the same inclination you could find no means of conversing with each other except at a window under cover of night. As it was afterwards told you used to be quite sorry when the sun rose. Your face looked bloodless, shrunken, and pale; and to remove all suspicion you used to be forever reading Christ's gospel as if you were a deacon indeed.[5]

Earlier Ambrosiaster had observed the powerful Roman deacons and saw two of them, Damasus and Ursinus,

---

5. St. Jerome, "To Sabinianus," *Ibid.*, p. 292.

struggling for the bishop's chair. He wrote trenchantly against the presumption of deacons. He agreed with Jerome that in the primitive Church bishops and presbyters were equal and deacons were in a lower order. Ambrosiaster argued that deacons were ministers to presbyters. "Someone named Fulcidius, influenced by his own stupidity and the illusions of the city of Rome, equated levites with priests and deacons with presbyters. . . . what audacity it is to make the ministers of presbyters their equals." Ambrosiaster corroborates the testimony of Jerome that the diaconate was already a preliminary step to the priesthood. The Roman Fulcidius was wrong when "he extolls deacons against presbyters, as if deacons were ordained from presbyters and not presbyters from deacons." Deacons were clearly inferior to higher orders. "What is a bishop unless just a presbyter, that is the high priest? He calls presbyters his fellow presbyters and fellow priests. He never calls deacons his fellow deacons. Never because they are clearly inferior." [6]

In the east deacons were "heralds of the church" who proclaimed the bidding prayers and directed the congregation. Deacons brought oblations to the altar and were responsible for the reading of the gospel, an honor that was not entrusted to lectors. At Rome deacons also chanted the elaborate graduals between epistle and gospel. As a result many Roman deacons were ordained because of their singing skill.

Augustine (d. 436), a disciple of Ambrose and correspondent of Jerome, wrote a whole treatise on catechetics in response to the request of a north African deacon. Deacons, therefore, although their prerogatives were under harsh attack, still served

---

6. Ambrosianus, "De Jactantia Romanarum Levitarum," PL, 3, 2302.

in the ministry of the word. The African deacon in question was reasonably well instructed but his ministry of the word consisted in rudimentary catechetics.

> You have asked me, brother Deogratias, to write something to you on the instructing of candidates for the catechumenate that may be of use to you. For you tell me that at Carthage where you are a deacon those who are to be grounded in the rudiments of the Christian faith are often brought to you because you are supposed to possess great ability in catechising, by reason both of your thorough training and the faith in the charm of your style.[7]

In Egypt St. Athanasius (d. 373) referred to the deacon's continuing role as mediator between bishop and faithful. Deacons kept the bishop informed of affairs pertinent to the episcopal office. "A certain Carpones, who had been excommunicated by Alexander for Arianism, was sent hither by one Gregory with certain others, also excommunicated for the same heresy. However, I had learned the matter also from the Presbyter Macarius, and the Deacons Martyrius and Hesychius" (Against the Arians, 24).[8] Deacons continued to serve as ambassadors for the bishop and informed him of affairs in other regions: "I wrote to my fellow ministers in Egypt, and sent a deacon, desiring to learn something of Arsenius, for

---

7. St. Augustine, *The First Catechetical Instruction*, (Ancient Christian Writers), Westminster, 1946, p. 13.

8. St. Athanasius, "Against the Arians," in *Select Writings and Letters of Athanasius, Bishop of Alexandria*, (NPNF), N.Y., 1892, p. 113.

I had not seen the man for five or six years" (65). The Egyptian bishop Alexander testified that "Athanasius sent his deacon into the Thebais, to search everywhere for Arsenius" (67).

At Jerusalem St. Cyril's lectures (347) give evidence of the deacon's role at the baptismal liturgy. Deacons assisted other ministers and in outlying regions sometimes administered the sacrament themselves.

> For at the season of baptism, when thou art come before the bishops, or presbyters, or deacons, — for its grace is everywhere, in village and in cities, on them of low and on them of high degree, on bondsmen and on freemen, (for this grace is not of men, but the gift is from God through men) — approach the Minister of Baptism, but approaching think not of the face of him thou seest, but remember the Holy Ghost of whom we are now speaking.[9]

St. John Chrysostom (d. 407), the great preacher of the East, was a sacerdotalist who stressed the similarity of bishops and priests; except for the power of ordination there was little difference between them. Deacons, however, were of a lower and temporary degree.

> ... between Presbyters and Bishops there was no great difference. Both had undertaken the office of Teachers and Presidents in the Church, and what he has said concerning Bishops is applicable to Presbyters. For they are only super-

---

9. St. Cyril of Jerusalem, "Lecture 17," in *The Catechetical Lectures of St. Cyril,* (NPNF), 1894, p. 132.

ior in having the power of ordination, and seem to have no other advantage over Presbyters.

Chrysostom interprets the author of 1 Timothy as teaching that the diaconate is a step to the priesthood. "They that use the office of a Deacon well, 'purchase to themselves a good degree,' that is advancement, 'and much boldness in the faith of Jesus Christ'; as if he would say, that those who have been found vigilant in the lower degree will soon ascend to the higher" (Homily 11).[10]

According to a fourth century liturgical work of the Egyptian bishop Serapion (d. 361) deacons assisted at the liturgy with bishops, presbyters, the minor orders, and laity. Deacons were to be pure in body and soul because of their ministry at the eucharistic liturgy. "Sanctify the deacons, too. May they be pure in body and soul and with a clear conscience do their service and watch over the holy body and the holy blood." In the ordination service there is a rite of "laying on of hands" for deacons, presbyters, and bishops. A prayer for deacons asks that they have knowledge and discernment for their service of God and his church among (and not above) the people.

O Father who sent us your only Son, you have appointed a place for everything on earth. You gave rules and laws to your church, in the interests of the flock and for its preservation. You chose bishops, priests and deacons for

10. St. John Chrysostom, "Homily 11," in *Homilies on Galatians, Ephesians, Philippians, Colossians, Thessalonicans, Timothy, Titus, and Philemon*, (NPNF), N.Y., 1889, p. 441.

the service of your Catholic Church. Through your Son you singled out seven deacons and you gave them the Holy Spirit. Appoint this servant, too, a deacon of your Catholic Church and give him the Spirit of knowledge and discernment, that he may be able to offer you pure and blameless service among your holy people, through your Son, Jesus Christ. Through him may glory and power be yours, now and age after age. Amen.[11]

The fourth and fifth century synods continued to legislate for deacons. The Council of Antioch (341) forbade deacons and presbyters to leave their local bishop; if they gathered schismatic congregations and erected an altar they were to be punished by the civil power (Canon 5). Chorepiscopi were forbidden to ordain deacons and presbyters without permission from the major bishop (10). No bishop could constitute presbyters and deacons subject to the jurisdiction of another bishop (22). Deacons assisted their bishop and presbyters in administration of church property (25).[12] At the Council of Carthage (390) the presiding bishop, Genethlius referred to deacons as "levites." Because of their service at the altar married deacons were to abstain from their wives (2). We observe the subordinate place of deacons when the Council legislates that bishops are to be judged by twelve of their peers, priests by six bishops, and deacons by three (13).[13]

---

11. "The Euchologium of Serapion" in *Early Christian Prayers*, Chicago, 1961, p. 122.

12. Mansi, 2, 1367.

13. Mansi, 3, 692-693.

A letter falsely attributed to Clement of Rome emphasized the deacon's role of mediation. As the "eyes of the bishop" deacons visited the sick and reported their needs to the bishop (Ep. 12).[14] Deacons were ministers of reconciliation who exhorted sinners to return to Church. As official mediators in the midst of the community they reported the physical and spiritual needs of God's people to the bishop who was, below God and Christ, the head of the church (Homily 3:67).

Socrates (d. 450), a church historian, testified that deacons were frequently nominated to the bishopric. We have observed Ambrosiaster's anger over the machinations of the Roman deacon Ursinus who was nominated but not elected bishop of Rome. Ursinus was a trouble-maker who fomented a local schism:

> A certain Ursinus, a deacon of that church, had been nominated among others when the election of a bishop took place: as Damasus was preferred this deacon, Ursinus, unable to bear the disappointment of his hopes, held schismatic assemblies apart from the church, and even induced certain bishops of little distinction to ordain him in secret (4:29).[15]

A Canon of Chalcedon (451) legislated for deaconesses in terms so similar to the Canons for clerics that it is difficult to maintain that women were not ordained to a female diaconate. "A woman less than forty years of age should not be ordained (*non ordinari*) deaconess; and this only with diligent

---

14. Pseudo-Clement, Epistle 12, PG, 2, 47.
15. *The Ecclesiastical History of Socrates,* (NPNF) Boston, 1890, p. 20.

probation; and if accepting ordination (*ordinationem*) and per-
severing some time in the ministry (*ministerio*), she hands her-
self over to marriage, condemning the grace of God, she is to be
anathematized with the man with whom she is joined." [16]

In Leo the Great's efficiently organized Rome (440-461)
deacons assisted the Pope as administrators and ambassadors.
The deacon who especially assisted the bishop became known
as archdeacon or "bishop's deacon." These men were often,
as in the time of Ambrosiaster, the second most important
persons in a diocese. Athanasius the archdeacon succeeded
Alexander as bishop of Alexandria in 328 and Dioscorus succeeded Cyril in 444. In 453 Pope Leo reprimanded Anatolius
of Constantinople "for degrading his archdeacon Aetius by
making him a presbyter." Ordinary deacons, no less than archdeacons, were invaluable assistants to the bishop. Adeodatus,
a deacon, reported to Leo the needs of the bishop of Aquileia:
". . . Adeodatus, a deacon of our See, reminds us of your
Charity's request that you receive from us the authoritative
answers of the Apostolic See about the matters which are apparently quite difficult to decide" [17] (Letter 159). Deacons conveyed letters for the bishop: "We received a letter from your
Charity through our son Basil the deacon" (35). "Basil the
deacon brought me your Clemency's letter" (104). "It was with
pleasure that I received your Fraternity's letter which Hermes
your archdeacon brought" (166). Deacons represented Pope
Leo at councils. Leo wrote to the bishops intending a council
at Ephesus: "I am sending our brothers, Julius the bishop,

---

16. Mansi, 6, 1225.

17. St. Leo the Great, *Letters*, (Fathers of the Church), N.Y., 1957,
p. 248.

Renatus the priest, and my son Hilary the deacon" (33). Hilary barely escaped that abortive "council" with his life: "Our son Hilary the deacon, refusing to be a party to the unjust sentence, had returned in flight. He had been sent with others to the council to represent us there" (50). In a famous letter Leo named his delegates to Chalcedon (451): "We are sending our brothers Julius the bishop and Renatus the priest, as well as my son Hilary the deacon to represent us in seeing that the entire problem is settled with piety toward and faith in God" (28).

There are indications in Leo's correspondence that even at Rome the diaconate was a preliminary step to higher orders. "He who is to be ordained priest or deacon may advance through all the ranks of the clerical order . . ." (8). Clerics advanced up the Roman hierarchy like officers in the army. It is noteworthy that Roman deacons could still marry — but only once. "He is still not to rise to the rank of the diaconate or to the priestly dignity or to the height of the bishopric if it is certain that he had married more than once or that his wife was previously married" (12). The ordination prayer for deacons included the following significant invocation: "That they may preserve firm and unwavering in Christ and by worthy steps through your grace they may merit to advance from a lower degree to a higher." [18]

According to Pseudo-Dionysius (c. 450) deacons served higher ministers at the liturgy. They introduced catechumens to doctrine and eventually to baptism. Soon their introductory *function* was applied to deacons themselves as the diaconate was

_____

18. PL 54, 115.

considered a final introductory step to the priesthood (Ecc. Hier.).[19] John Cassian (d. 450), in the *Collations,* mentioned a deacon who was ordained to the priesthood by a presbyter.[20]

The historian Philostorghius (d. 439) testifies that deacons still preached. One deacon, Aetius, contributed to the demise of diaconal preaching by his venture in "ecclesiastical dogmatics." Reportedly, Leontius, bishop of Antioch, "when he was raised to the episcopate of Antioch, ordained his disciple to the diaconate, and permitted him to preach ecclesiastical dogmatics publicly in church" (Eccl. Hist. 3: 17).[21] Unfortunately Aetius took all too readily to the role of preacher. He neglected the diaconal function of charity and became involved in the rarefied christological debates of his time. Under the influence of the heretic Eunomius he preached Arian subordinationism. Despite the mishaps of Aetius, late writers had kind words for deacons who were compared to angelic orders. Because of their angelic functions deacons wore white albs at liturgy.[22]

Early medieval canons repeated the now familiar refrain that "deacons of the church are like the eyes of the bishop," because they mediated the needs of the diocese to the bishop. They still enjoyed the important responsibility of ministry to the sick: "Deacons solicitously seek out those who are sick, and if the laity are ignorant of their needs the deacons report these needs that the faithful may visit them and bring them

---

19. Pseudo-Dionysius, *Ecclesiastica Hierarchia,* PG, 3, 524, 508, 544.
20. Cassianus, *Collationes,* PL, 49, 583-585.
21. Philostorghius, *Ecclesiastical History,* PG, 65, 508-509.
22. Sophrynius, *Liturgical Commentary, PG,* 82, 3987.

the necessities of life." The canons emphasized the introductory role of deacons who were responsible for visitors, the maintenance of the altar, and ancillary roles at liturgy. They are also exhorted to be skillful in catechetics: "Those who catechize, that is, those who instruct beginners, should first be well instructed themselves; for they are dealing with the souls of men. It behooves him who instructs simple people to be such that he is able to adapt himself to the capacity of his listeners and to arrange his teaching for the capacity of his hearers" [23] (Codex of Ecclesiastical Canons, 64, 460-461).

According to an anonymous fifth century compilation entitled *Testament of Our Lord* deacons were "men of good conduct, chosen for purity and for abstinence from distractions, not entangled in the business of the world." There were customarily seven deacons in a church: "In the church let there be twelve presbyters, seven deacons, fourteen subdeacons, thirteen widows who sit in front . . . ." The deacons served in union with their bishop. The *Testament of Our Lord* emphasized the deacon's role of charity.

> Let him be the counsellor of the whole clergy, and the mystery of the Church; who ministereth to the sick, who ministereth to the strangers, who helpeth the widows, who is the father of the orphans, who goeth about all the houses of those that are in need, lest any be in affliction or sickness or misery. Let him go about in the houses of the catechumens, so that he may confirm those who are doubting and teach those who are unlearned.
>
> Let him clothe those men who have departed, adorning

---

23. *Codex of Ecclesiastical Canons*, PL, 56, 736-737.

(them); burying the strangers; guiding those who pass from their dwelling, or go into captivity. For the help of those who are in need let him notify the Church; let him not trouble the bishop; but only on the first day of the week let him make mention about everything, so that he may know.[24]

A council at Vaison (442) concerned itself with the friction between deacons and presbyters. The council stipulated that in the absence of a presbyter deacons were to read homilies of the Fathers. The council fathers felt compelled to defend this function of deacons.

If the presbyter, hindered by some infirmity, is not himself able to preach, let homilies of the fathers be recited by deacons. For if deacons are worthy to read the words of Christ in the gospels, why are they judged unworthy to recite publicly the expositions of the holy fathers? [25]

The *Statuta Ecclesiae Antiquae,* (c. 480) a collection of early legislation, is vigorously pro-presbyter and almost hostile to deacons. According to the *Statutes,* "the deacon should acknowledge himself minister of the presbyter as well as the bishop"; "the deacon, in the presence of a presbyter, in cases of necessity and if he is ordered, may distribute the Eucharist of the body of Christ to the people"; "the deacon is to sit when the presbyter commands"; "the deacon is to use the alb only

---

24. *Testament of Our Lord,* James Cooper, ed., (Ante-Nicene Christian Library), Edinburgh, 1902, pp. 97-99.
25. Mansi, 8, 727.

at the time of oblations and the reading"; "in a gathering of presbyters, when the deacon is questioned, let him speak." [26]

Despite the *Statutes'* restrictions, Roman deacons and archdeacons were visible at the liturgy, in ministry of the word, and in works of charity, including administration. These Cardinal deacons, as we may begin to designate them, also represented the Pope at the imperial court. The deacon Pelagius represented Pope Vigilius at the court of Justinian. When Vigilius died in 554 Pelagius succeeded him as Pope. Pope Gregory (590-604) objected when cantors were ordained to the diaconate. He forbade deacons to sing at liturgy. They were to *read* the gospel.

A very reprehensible custom has arisen whereby certain cantors are chosen for the ministry of the altar and are constituted in the order of deacons for the modulation of their voice . . . in this See ministers of the altar are not to sing, and during mass let them only read the gospel. Psalms and other readings should be recited by subdeacons or, if necessary, by those in minor orders.[27]

The power of archdeacons was an irritant not only to presbyters but even to some bishops. To diminish the power of the archdeacon Honoratus, his bishop, Natalis, nominated him for the presbyterate. Honoratus preferred not to be "kicked upstairs" and found a powerful supporter in Pope Gregory who wrote a letter "to induce Natalis, our brother and fellow bishop,

---

26. *Statuta Ecclesiae Antiquae,* Charles Munier, ed., Paris, 1950, pp. 89-90.

27. Mansi, 9, 1226.

who has been admonished by so many letters, to restore the above-mentioned Honoratus to his place immediately" (Ep. 20).[28]

Deacons still sought and won the bishop's chair. Pope Gregory testified that "on the death of Laurentius, bishop of the church of Milan, the clergy reported to us that they had unanimously agreed in the election of our son, Constantine, their deacon" (Ep. 30).

The councils of the early Middle Ages frequently stipulated the twenty-fifth year as the minimum age for ordination to the diaconate. The French Council of Agde (506) decreed that married deacons should separate from their wives before ordination. They were to be twenty-five years of age for ordination to the diaconate and thirty for the presbyterate. "The bishop should not commit the blessing of the diaconate to those under twenty-five years . . . let no one presume to ordain a presbyter or bishop before thirty years, that is, before he comes to the age of the perfect man." [29]

Even as the permanent diaconate faded many deacons still served in that order for five or more years. Venerable Bede, himself a deacon for eleven years,[30] wrote of the deacon James whom Bishop Paulinus (d. 644) left behind at York. "He left behind him, in his church at York, James the deacon, a holy ecclesiastic, who continuing long after in that church, by

---

28. *The Letters and Sermons of Gregory the Great*, (NPNF), N.Y., 1895, p. 105.

29. Mansi, 8, 327.

30. *The Venerable Bede's Ecclesiastical History, also The Anglo-Saxon Chronicle*, J. A. Giles, ed., London, 1890, pp. XI-XII.

teaching and baptizing, rescued much prey from the power of the old enemy of mankind." [31]

In the imaginative literature of the seventh century, deacons, presbyters, and bishops were compared to Christ; but deacons were compared to Christ in his more lowly roles of service. Not surprisingly, then, deacons served presbyters as well as bishops. The fourth council of Toledo (633) under Isidore of Seville, stated, "It is forbidden for a bishop or presbyter to use two oraria, how much more for a deacon who is their servant." [32]

In the ordination prayers of the *Gelasian Sacramentary,* which circulated widely in seventh and eighth century Gaul, the diaconate was a preliminary step to higher orders: "May they persevere firm and stable in Christ, and by worthy steps by your grace may they advance from a lower grade to a higher." As had been the custom since Hippolytus only the bishop imposed hands at the ordination of a deacon "because he is consecrated not for the priesthood but for ministry." Deacons were Christian "levites" whose function was almost exclusively liturgical. [33]

But ecclesiastical writers tried to make these liturgical functions important and even indispensable. Isidore (d. 636), for example, claimed that without the ministry of deacons —

a priest has the name, he does not have the office. The priest consecrates, the deacon dispenses the sacrament.

---

31. *Bede's Ecclesiastical History of the English Nation,* London, 1951, pp. 102-103.

32. Mansi, 10, 629.

33. *The Gelasian Sacramentary,* H. A. Wilson, ed., Oxford, 1844, 26-27, 146-149. Cf. PL, 82, 892.

The priest prays, the deacon recites the psalms. The priest sanctifies the oblations, the deacon dispenses what has been sanctified. It is not permitted for priests through their presumption to take the chalice from the table of the Lord unless it is handed to them by a deacon.[34]

An anonymous writer, in a treatise on the seven orders, repeats the words of Isidore and adds: "The priest needs the office of the deacon just as the deacon needs the office of the priest; a rich man cannot exist without the poor, nor the poor without the rich." [35]

In eighth century Ireland, and later on the continent, the deacon was compared to Christ washing his disciples' feet, the priest to Christ consecrating the bread and wine at the Last Supper, and the bishop to Christ solemnly blessing the apostles.[36] The Diaconate, while it was an important rank within the seven orders, was primarily liturgical. There were, however, occasional references to deacons who administered church property. A German council in 745 reported that "false presbyters and fornicating deacons and clerics we have removed from the money of the churches and degraded and compelled to penance." [37]

A ninth century florilegium, connected with southern Germany but resembling the imaginative literature of Ireland, nar-

---

34. Isidore, *De Ecclesiasticis Officiis*, PL, 83, 788-789.
35. Pseudo-Jerome, *Epistle XII, De Septem Ordinibus*, PL, 30, 153-154.
36. "Les Ordres du Christ," *Revue Des Sciences Religieuses*, Vol. 3, No. 1, (1923), p. 309.
37. Mansi, 12, 366.

rates that Christ "was Deacon when he washed the feet of his disciples. He was priest when he took bread and blessed it. He was bishop when he raised his hands and blessed his disciples." [38] The same document reveals again that the medieval deacon's role was primarily liturgical. "It behooves the deacon to minister at the altar and to baptize . . . . The minister is called levite or deacon because he ministers at the altar to the priest offering. He places the oblations on the altar; and he dispenses the sanctified oblations. A priest without a deacon has the name, he does not have the office." The deacon's liturgical ministry was considered important; he was assisted by subdeacons. "The subdeacon is so called because he is subject to the deacon, carrying the oblations from the people to the deacon at the altar for placing on the altar of God." [39]

Because of the diaconal ministry at the altar ninth century canonical legislation forbade deacons to attend weddings or other festivals where erotic canticles were sung. The canons forbade house masses but allowed deacons to assist priests at certain exceptional liturgies such as mass in a convent.[40] Presbyters were forbidden to enter convents without a deacon. They heard confessions of women only in church "excepting the infirm in whose homes it is necessary to do it. To avoid scandal, let the presbyter have with him a deacon and subdeacon of good reputation, by whom he may be seen, and his reputation will be protected." [41]

---

38. Roger Reynolds, "A Florilegium on the Ecclesiastical Grades in CLM 19414," *Harvard Theological Review*, Vol. 63, No. 2. (April, 1970), p. 251.

39. *Ibid.*, 252.

40. Mansi, 14, 340.

41. Mansi, 14, 276.

4

By the tenth century almost everywhere in the west the diaconate was a temporary and ceremonial order in the hierarchy. As if to compensate for his diminished role the literature of the late Middle Ages frequently argued that the deacon's ancillary functions were essential for an authentic liturgical act. Presbyters were forbidden to baptize without the assistance of a deacon. The tenth century chapters of Otto, bishop of Vercelli, stipulated that presbyters were to spare no effort in acquiring the services of a deacon.

Whence every presbyter not having a deacon should choose some one and make him known to his people. Then he should introduce him to the bishop. When he is approved he will be consecrated. If the presbyter does not bring one forward, saying he does not have such a cleric, his bishop will provide a good person from his own church or elsewhere. It is important that there should be a deacon.[42]

The Sentences of Peter Lombard (d. 1160) summarized the role of the deacon as we have seen it develop in the Middle Ages. Lombard repeated traditional teaching: deacons were levites of the new dispensation, assistants to Christian "priests"; their role was primarily liturgical, but he did not overlook their traditional ministry of the word and of charity.

These are called deacons in Greek, ministers in Latin because just as in the priest consecration, so also in the deacon dispensation of the mystery. It pertains to deacons to assist priests and to minister in all things which are done in the

---

42. PL, 134, 32.

sacraments of Christ; that is, in baptism, in chrism, in the paten and chalice, to carry the oblations and place them on the altar, to take care of and decorate the table of the Lord; to carry the cross, and to read the epistle and gospel to the people. Just as lectors in the Old Testament, the deacons of the New are ministers of the word. To deacons also pertains the recitation of prayer and the reading of names of new catechumens. The deacon admonishes all to hear the Lord; he gives the peace and he announces . . . deacons receive the texts of the gospel that they may know themselves to be preachers of the gospel of Christ.[43]

Lombard testified to the continuation of the custom extending back into the second century whereby "only the bishop imposes hands on them because they are applied to the ministry." Similarly, he reiterated the exegesis, traditional since Irenaeus, which traced the origin of the diaconate to the appointment of the seven hellenists by the twelve apostles. The number seven was in the Middle Ages the diaconal number. There were to be seven deacons in a church; they were compared to the seven angels in the Apocalypse.

The Sentences of Bandinus include a treatise on ecclesiastical orders which summarizes succinctly the medieval role of the diaconate.

The order of deacons is in the sixth place in which their perfection is commended. In Latin these are called ministers because just as in the priest consecration, so in the deacons there is dispensation of the mysteries. It pertains to

---

43. Peter Lombard, *Sentences*, PL, 192, 903.

the deacon to care for the altar, to carry the cross, and to preach, and always to assist and minister to those giving the sacraments. They are also called levites, from the tribe of Levi, because just as the ministration of the temple for the whole people was committed to that tribe, so the ministry of the altar for the whole church is committed to these ministers. The bishop places his hand on them when they are ordained and puts a stole on the left shoulder that they might be prepared to minister . . . he also gives them a text of the gospel so that he may anoint them to be preachers of Christ.[44]

Peter Cantor (d. 1191), an influential sacramental theologian, emphasized the diaconal role at liturgy, but he cautioned against the misunderstanding that deacons were absolutely necessary for the celebration of the Eucharist. "As a secretary at the altar he shares with the priest in the confection of the Eucharist; not because he takes or consecrates or because the Eucharist cannot be confected without him, but because the body and blood of Christ is consecrated more fittingly and with greater reverence with the deacon's presence, ministry, and testimony." [45]

In general the late medieval archdeacons were legal representatives of the bishop and were not always deacons in fact. Many were not ordained to the diaconate; others were worldly. An outstanding example is Thomas of London, archdeacon to Archbishop Theobald of Canterbury. When Thomas

---

44. Bandinus, *Sentences*, PL, 192, 1104.
45. PL, 201, 184.

became chancellor to Henry II he was known as a worldly companion to the king. Only when he was ordained to the priesthood on the day before his consecration to the episcopate (1162) did Becket change his character from worldling to saint. Yet in many areas archdeacons were still ecclesiastics to be reckoned with. They administered some dioceses and summoned grave sinners to repentance; at ordination they led approved ordinands to the bishop. A twelfth century French synod forbade presbyters "to receive chaplaincies without the knowledge of the bishop or archdeacon." [46] Deacons, however, were told to keep their place. Once again they were forbidden to hear confessions: "It is strictly forbidden for deacons to hear confessions, except in the gravest necessity; for they neither have the keys nor can they absolve." [47] Only in grave necessity could deacons administer communion to the sick: "Let presbyters not permit deacons . . . to carry the sacred body of the Lord to the sick, except in necessity, when a priest is unavailable." [48]

In the thirteenth century the synod of Pictavia (1280) again legislated against the practice of deacons hearing confessions. Deacons who continued to pronounce absolution would be excommunicated: "Wishing to eradicate an erroneous abuse that has arisen in our diocese from pernicious ignorance we forbid that deacons hear confessions or absolve in the penitential forum, since it is certain that they are not able to absolve, since they do not have the keys which are conferred solely to the sacerdotal order." [49]

---

46. PL, 212, 68.
47. *Ibid.*
48. PL, 212, 60.
49. Mansi, 24, 383-384.

For St. Thomas Aquinas (d. 1274) whose writings exerted enormous influence on the theology and practice of subsequent centuries, deacons were clearly inferior to bishops and presbyters.[50] According to Thomas, what pertains to an ecclesiastical order can be deduced from the name of that order. "Deacons are called ministers because it does not pertain to deacons principally and *ex officio* to confect a sacrament but to minister to higher orders in the performance of sacraments." Deacons enjoyed the power of reading the gospel and preaching: "It pertains to the deacon to read the gospel in church and to preach catechetically." But deacons could not baptize *ex officio*: "It does not pertain to a deacon as from his proper office to give the sacrament of baptism, but to assist in the administration of this sacrament and to minister to higher orders."[51] Since baptism was necessary for salvation, in urgent necessity deacons could baptize: "Because baptism is a necessary sacrament deacons are permitted to baptize in urgent necessity when higher orders are not present."[52]

St. Thomas argued that deacons could not administer extreme unction *even in urgent necessity*. The diaconate was compared to the purgative way; and since the dispensation of sacramental grace pertained to the illuminative way the deacon *ex officio* did not administer sacraments. "The deacon has purgative force only, not illuminative. Therefore, since illumination happens through grace the deacon *ex officio* cannot confect

---

50. St. Thomas Aquinas, *Summa Theologiae Supplementum Tertiae Partis*, q. 40, art. 5, ad. 2.
51. *Summa Theologiae Tertiam Partem*, q. 67, art. 1.
52. *Ibid.*, ad. 1-3.

a sacrament in which grace is conferred. And so he cannot administer this sacrament (extreme unction) because grace is conferred." Since extreme unction, unlike baptism, was not a necessary sacrament, "its dispensation in necessity is not committed to everyone but only to those to whom it belongs *ex officio.*" [53]

Those in holy orders were obliged to continence — because holy orders were concerned with holy things. Sexual intercourse was considered incompatible with the sacralized ministry of the altar.

> An order is called holy in two ways. First, in itself. And so every order is holy because it is a sacrament in some way. Secondly, by reason of the matter concerning which it has some action. And so an order is called holy because it has an action concerning some sacred thing. And so there are only three holy orders, namely, the priest, and the deacon who has actions concerning the consecrated body and blood of Christ, and the subdeacon who has an action concerning the consecrated vessels. Therefore, continence is indicated for them so that they who are concerned with holy things may be clean.[54]

At ordination priests, deacons, and subdeacons received the blessing because all three orders were commissioned for divine service. Priests and deacons received imposition of

---

53. *Supplementum Tertiae Patris,* q. 30, art. 1.
54. *Ibid.,* q. 37, art. 3.

hands because these two orders were empowered to dispense sacraments. Priests alone were anointed because only their order confected sacraments *ex officio* and they alone touched the body and blood of Christ.

> Through the blessing they are committed to divine services. And so the blessing is bestowed upon all. But through imposition of hands there is given a fullness of grace through which they are suitable for great offices. And so imposition of hands is done only to priests and deacons because the dispensation of sacraments is in their competence; although to one as principal, to the other as minister. But by unction someone is consecrated for confecting a sacrament. And so unction is done only to priests because with their own hands they touch the body of Christ.[55]

The diaconal power, according to St. Thomas, was midway between that of the priest and subdeacon. In his description of this "power" and the bestowal of the "character" we observe that major orders were considered mainly in relation to the Eucharist; the deacon's ministry was almost exclusively liturgical.

> The power of the deacon is midway between the power of the priest and that of the subdeacon. The priest directly has power over the body of Christ; the subdeacon, however, over the vessels only, but the deacon over the body contained in the vessel. Therefore it is not for him to touch

---

55. *Ibid.*, q. 37, art. 5.

the body of Christ but to carry the body in the paten, and to dispense the blood with the chalice. And so his power for the principal action cannot be expressed through the bestowal of the vessel only nor through the bestowal of the matter. But his power for the secondary act is expressed in this that the book of gospels is given to him; and in this power the other is understood. And so in the very giving of the book the character is impressed.[56]

Women, according to the scholastics, were inferior to males. They were incapable of receiving the sacrament of orders, "Since therefore in the feminine sex there cannot be signified some eminence of grade, because the woman has the state of subjection, so she is unable to receive the sacrament of order." [57]

The role of the deacon on the eve of the reformation was subordinate, temporary, and almost wholly liturgical. His was a preliminary albeit ascending grade in a pseudo-Dionysian hierarchy. The permanence and importance that had once been his had all but vanished. Many of his original functions had been assumed by members of religious communities. The theology of order concentrated on the relation of orders to the Eucharist; and eucharistic theology was mainly concerned with the real presence in the elements. The deacon's role was to assist bishops and priests in the liturgy.

But the historic reality of the diaconate never died out. Temporary deacons continued to assist at liturgy, to read the

---

56. *Ibid.*, ad. 5.
57. *Ibid.*, q. 39, art. 1.

gospel, to preach, and on occasion to perform services of charity. There were deacons in the monasteries and, despite the strictures of Gregory the Great, deacons continued to chant in church. Moreover, late medieval legislation permitted deacons to remain in the order for several years. The archdiaconate, one of the historic causes of friction between deacons and presbyters, persevered at Rome until modern times. In the great and separated churches of the East permanent deacons still functioned, although even in the East the diaconal ministry was mainly liturgical.

Nor can we say that the permanent diaconate ever wholly vanished in the Latin West. Francis Assisi had no intentions of seeking the priesthood when he was "tonsured" and commissioned to preach.[58] At Pentecost, 1218, when Cardinal Hugolin chanted mass for the Friars in the Portiuncula "Francis officiated as deacon and read the gospel." [59] When the little poor man of Assisi died in 1226 he had been a cleric for sixteen years. He never became a priest.

In the last will and testament of Francis we have a vivid example of the sacralization of Christian priesthood which was a major reason for the decline in importance of the diaconate. As long as a priest "consecrated" he was valuable and sacred. The deacon was wholly inferior to those who touched the body and blood of Christ. In his will Francis wrote:

> Even though I had all the wisdom of Solomon, if I should find poor secular priests, I would not preach in their

---

58. Johannes Jorgensen, *St. Francis of Assisi*, N.Y., 1913, pp. 97-98.
59. *Ibid.*, p. 194.

parishes without their consent . . . I will not consider their sins, for in them I see the Son of God and they are my Lords. I do this because here below I see nothing, I perceive nothing corporally of the most high Son of God, if not His most holy Body and Blood, which they receive and they alone distribute to others.[60]

As urbanization accelerated so did the rise of merchants and burghers. Services of charity, once the prerogative of deacons, were assumed by secular organizations. This, too, contributed to the eclipse of the ecclesiastical diaconal function. As Yves Congar notes, "From the late Middle Ages (the rising urban class) had been taking the place of clerics in various duties formerly discharged by the Church, notably in works of charity." [61]

The diaconate that confronted the reformers and Trent was temporary, subordinate, mainly ceremonial. In returning to scripture and the primitive Church the reformers realized the value of the diaconal function within the official ordering of the Church. They took steps to restore the diaconal function so that the Church could bring reconciliation to the alienated citizens of the cities.

In their epoch the reformers encountered a diaconate reduced merely to a fixed ceremonial institution without any rapport with the practical necessities of life of communities.

---

60. Quoted in Paul Sabatier, *St. Francis of Assisi*, N.Y., 1917, pp. 337-338.

61. Yves Congar, *Lay People in the Church*, N.Y., 1956, pp. 35-36.

Therefore their intent to restore the diaconate was primarily concerned with these practical necessities, that is, with the responsibility of the Christian community toward its suffering members.[62]

But in the mother Church of Rome the diaconate was to remain temporary, subordinate, and ceremonial until the Roman Catholic reformation of the twentieth century.

---

62. Herbert Krim, "Le Diacre Dans Les Eglises Protestantes," in *Le Diacre Dans Le Monde,* p. 75. For the diaconate in Protestant, Anglican, and Orthodox churches see *Ibid.,* pp. 75-140.

Trent to the Restoration: The Deacon Returns

As the reformation swept across northern Europe Catholic as well as Protestant reformers sought to repristinate the diaconate. The sick, aged, and indigent of splintering Christendom suffered for lack of the diaconal ministry. Catholic, Lutheran and especially reformed churches struggled to bring the diaconate in line with the early Church so that deacons could again serve human needs. Within the wounded Church of Rome theologians as well as humanists were aware of the once golden age of the diaconate; many of them advocated a restoration of primitive diaconal functions.

But when a reforming council finally gathered at Trent in 1545 the prospects for restored permanence of the diaconate or even a meaningful ministry of the word in "lower" ministers were not bright. Some council fathers were aware of Ambrosiaster's attack on Roman deacons — and only recently had scholars demonstrated that Ambrosiaster's polemics did not come from the pen of the great Ambrose.[1] Another early adversary of deacons was Jerome, the respected translator of the Vulgate which Trent recognized as the "authentic" version. While few Tridentine fathers were as familiar with Jerome as

1. Piet Fransen, "Divorce on the Ground of Adultery — the Council of Trent," *The Future of Marriage As Institution*, Franz Bockle, ed., (The New Concilium), N.Y., 1970.

was the humanist Erasmus who "was better acquainted with Jerome and Seneca than with his own prior," [2] there were many at Trent who shared Jerome's fears of a powerful diaconate. Moreover, the teachings of St. Thomas were revered by those with scholastic predilection and, as we have seen, Thomas was less than generous to deacons.

Sacerdotalism, partly in reaction to Protestant attacks on the priesthood and mass, was a major factor militating against revival of the diaconate. James Laynez, the Jesuit General who was originally sent to Trent by Pope Paul III, spoke harshly against a proposal that deacons should preach. "The devil induces the legislation of those things which destroy the priesthood under pretext, that a deacon should preach and other things of this kind." [3]

There was also grave concern at Trent about the abuses of pluralism and the ordination of minors. To cite one prominent example, Charles Borromeo before his "conversion" was a "beneficed clergyman at the age of twelve, a pluralist and an archbishop at the uncanonical age of twenty one, a Cardinal at twenty two . . . ." [4] When callow scions were ordained to the lower clergy and given benefices some of the understandable resentment was directed at deacons. At Trent the Archbishop of Rheims lamented the abuse "in deacon Cardinals who were sometimes ordained at the age of twelve and given churches

---

2. Roland Bainton, *Erasmus of Christendom*, N.Y., 1969, p. 19.

3. *Concilium Tridentinum: Diariorum, actorum, epistolarum, tractatuum, nova collectio*, Görres-Gesellschaft, Freiburg, 1901, 9, p. 589.

4. Owen Chadwick, *The Reformation*, Baltimore, 1964, p. 284.

which should not be given except to those of the mature age of thirty." [5] The Archbishop of Venice argued that "the age for subdeacons and deacons should be observed even in the creation of Cardinals." [6] Another father argued that "what is said about the quality and age of lower grades should also be declared about Cardinals, and those who are not priests should not be made bishops." [7]

The diaconate did not arise as a major or divisive issue during the deliberations at Trent and Bologna. The diaconate had declined — and it seemed destined to remain a temporary and ceremonial step to the priesthood. What concerned the Tridentine fathers were the issues of doctrine and reform.

But the question of the diaconate *did* emerge. If the council was to reform the Church of Rome this could be done not by returning to the Middle Ages but by conformity to scripture and the early Church. And an active diaconate was evident in scripture and the early Church. There were, moreover, pressing needs for the Church's charity as Europe urbanized.[8]

In June, 1563, the bishop of Ostuni called for the restoration of subdiaconal and diaconal functions. His brief remarks reveal a penetrating knowledge of the early diaconate as well as

---

5. *Concilium Tridentinum*, 9, p. 492.

6. *Ibid.*, p. 540.

7. *Ibid.*, p. 560.

8. Anglican deacons cooperated with the government in ministrations to the poor in the cities of Elizabethan England. Cf. *English Economic History — Select Documents*, A. E. Bland, ed., London, 1914, pp. 369-371.

keen sensitivity to the needs for diaconal charity in the sixteenth century.

I desire the function of the subdeacon and deacon, diligently collected from the writings of the fathers and decrees of the councils, to be restored and put to use, especially the functions of deacons. The Church has always used their services, not only in ministering at the altar, but in baptism, in care of hospitals, of widows, and of suffering persons. Finally, all the needs and concerns of the people are mediated to the bishop by deacons.[9]

This same prelate recommended a longer interval between major orders, "at least three or four years," in effect the establishment of a temporary "permanent" diaconate.[10] The bishop of Assisi urged that "deacons should not be ordained except for a certain benefice." [11] Another father requested that "the functions of these orders be restored." [12]

But as we have seen there was formidable sentiment against broadening the diaconal function. At a congregation of theologians the Jesuit Salmeron contended (against earlier synodal legislation) that the diaconate was instituted not for service of profane tables but for ministry at the altar!

Those deacons therefore were not instituted for ministry

---

9. *Concilium Tridentinum,* 9, p. 558.
10. *Ibid.,* pp. 558-559.
11. *Ibid.,* p. 535; cf. p. 536.
12. *Ibid.,* p. 511.

of profane tables but heavenly. For the ministry of profane tables there was no need that, before deacons were constituted, they should fast, they should impose hands, they should be filled with the Holy Spirit. Those deacons therefore were chosen for ministering the eucharist.... [13]

Benedict of Mantua, a Dominican argued that the diaconate was a sacrament because according to "Ambrose" and Ignatius deacons were "not to minister at profane tables but sacred." [14] Francis Sancius, dean of the faculty of theology at Salamanca, was aware that "the seven" Jerusalem hellenists were indeed ordained for ministry at *profane* tables but he contended their *principal* function was ministry at the altar. "There are seven orders of which the first, that is priests, deacons, and sub-deacons, are called major because they are principally concerned wtih the Eucharist and are called holy . . . the seven deacons in Acts 6 were instituted not only for profane tables but for spiritual tables." [15] A draft composed by the great Augustinian Cardinal and legate, Seripando, described lower orders as temporary and ascending; minor orders ascend through higher until "they are consummated in the priesthood." [16]

There were numerous fathers, in addition to James Laynez, who voiced opposition to preaching by deacons. In the voting

---

13. *Ibid.*, p. 7.
14. *Ibid.*, p. 13.
15. *Ibid.*, p. 11.
16. *Ibid.*, p. 41.

on a canon which proposed that deacons should preach the bishop of Calvi said, "It displeases that deacons should be held to preach." [17] In this he was supported by the bishop of Troia who stated, "It displeases where it is said that deacons should be held to preach." [18] The bishop of Gaudix reacted even more pointedly, "It pleases, after the expression is removed which says the deacon may preach the word of God." The Italian bishop Bellomo voted "*placet*" on condition that the provisions for diaconal preaching would be deleted.[19] There was already unseemly friction between seculars and mendicants about preaching the word of God. Some fathers were reluctant to complicate matters further by granting this faculty to deacons.[20]

However, on July 6, 1563, the council considered a detailed text on the entire ministry. A paragraph on the diaconate betrays a surprising sensitivity to the potential of the diaconate. The fact that this paragraph was submitted is in itself significant. It reads as follows:

It is clear how many and necessary and sacred were the services committed to the order of deacons which is distinct from other orders and the next to the priesthood. They are the eyes of the bishops and special ministers of the church whose office of celebration of sacred mysteries and care

---

17. *Ibid.*, p. 564.
18. *Ibid.*
19. *Ibid.*, p. 535; cf. pp. 548, 565.
20. Hubert Jedin, *A History of the Council of Trent*, 2 vols., St. Louis, 1961, Vol. II, p. 101.

of the church should never be lacking. And in the holy
sacrifice they offer at the altar the oblations received from
the subdeacon. They care for the table of God. They announce the gospel to the people. They assist the consecrating priests. They admonish the people about the solemn
rites to be observed in church. They ought to exhort that
these raise their hearts and prepare their souls for prayer,
and to warn those who intend to be present at the sacrifice
to have no adversity among themselves, not hatred, not
wrath nor ill will, but mutual charity. The ministry of
deacons should be diligent in governing the church. Their
office is to guard the preaching bishop lest he be approached
by vicious enemies or the divine word be reviled by insults
and despised. When the bishop so directs it pertains to
deacons to baptize and preach, also to reconcile to the
church public penitents in case of necessity and in the
absence of the bishop and priests, providing they reconcile
without solemnity. Deacons should seek out and care for
with zeal whatever pertains to the corporal assistance of
widows, of students, of orphans, of incarcerated, of sick
and all afflicted persons, and provide for the spiritual
help of the faithful. They have loving concern for all the
faithful in works of mercy, especially for those in whom
they observe a greater need for their charity.

Therefore this sacred synod considers all these things
so necessary that bishops should take care that those things
which have been done to this day should be holily and
religiously continued. Let them restore with zeal those which
were interrupted by negligence, so that the faithful, with

the help of God, may more easily attain eternal beatitude.[21]

When the council voted on orders, the chapter asserted that "The sacred scriptures make open mention not only of priests, but also deacons: and teach, in words the most weighty, what things are to be attended to in the ordination thereof." [22] A corresponding canon says: "If anyone says that beside the priesthood there are not in the Catholic Church other orders, both major and minor, by which, as by certain steps, advance is made to the priesthood, let him be anathema." [23] The diaconate therefore was a step to the priesthood. Another canon lumped deacons with other *"ministri"*: "If anyone says that in the Catholic Church there is not a hierarchy instituted by divine ordination, consisting of bishops, priests, and ministers, let him be anathema." [24] The council left open the question of the explicit divine institution of the hierarchy. But the ambiguous use of *"ministri"* would lead to considerable debate until Pius XII and, later, Vatican II settled the question: *deacons* and not other ministers of lower grade were within the hierarchy.

In the decree "On Reformation" the council proposed the minimal age for ordination to the diaconate as twenty three, and for the priesthood twenty five. Deacons were to be ordained to the priesthood after they "have served in their office of

---

21. *Concilium Tridentinum*, 9, p. 601.

22. *Enchiridion Symbolorum Definitionum et Declarationum de rebus fidei et morum*, Henricus Denzinger and Adolfus Schonmetzer, eds., 23rd edition, N.Y., 1965, p. 413 (1772).

23. *Ibid.*, p. 414 (1765).

24. *Ibid.*, p. 414 (1776).

deacon during at least an entire year unless for the utility and necessity of the Church the bishop shall judge otherwise." [25]

In this same decree the council directed prelates to restore the pristine *functions* of the diaconate and minor orders. Only clerics within these orders were to exercise the specific functions of their order — and they were to be supported from ecclesiastical revenues.

> That the function of holy orders — from the deacon to the janitor — which functions have been laudably received in the Church from the times of the apostles, and which have been for some time interrupted in very many places — may be again brought into use in accordance with the sacred canons, and that they may not be traduced by heretics as useless; the holy Synod, burning with the desire of restoring the pristine usage, ordains that, for the future, such functions shall not be exercised but by those who actually are in the said orders; and it exhorts in the Lord all and each of the prelates of the church and commands them, that it be their care to restore the said functions, as far as it can conveniently be done, in the Cathedral, Collegiate, and parochial churches of their dioceses, where the number of the people and the revenues of the church can support it. . . .[26]

But this directive was never really implemented until after Vatican II. In the centuries between these councils the role of the deacon remained subordinate, temporary, and mainly

---

25. *The Canons and Decrees of the Council of Trent,* J. Waterworth, ed., and trans., London, 1848, p. 185 (Decree on reformation).

26. *Ibid.,* pp. 186-187.

liturgical. Pristine diaconal functions despite the ordination of Trent were exercised by persons not in the diaconal order.[27] The insignificant place of the deacon in the post-Tridentine Church was finally codified in the 1917 Code of Canon Law.

The canonical age for ordination to the diaconate was twenty two, for the priesthood twenty four (CIC 975). Before ordination to the diaconate the candidate was to have begun his fourth year of theology (976:2). He was to remain at least three months in the diaconate unless the bishop decides otherwise (978:3). In some religious communities clerics remained deacons for only one day—a privilege clearly manifesting the eclipse of the historic diaconate. In June, 1961, this writer was a deacon for four days, an interval between major orders that was considered extraordinarily long at the time.

While the faculty of preaching was granted to deacons (1342), in practice very few deacons ascended the pulpit. Priests and occasionally bishops did most of the preaching. Admittedly, with the reform of seminary training that followed Trent the ministry of the word was more professional than in the Middle Ages. Seculars as well as regulars were able to preach. But after graduation from the seminary many priests became apostles of activism. As a result many parish priests woefully neglected the continuing study of scripture, homiletics,

---

27. It should be remembered that the permanent diaconate continued to function in many eastern communities and was restored in various forms in reformation churches. To cite but one example, in 1625 William Laud ordained Nicholas Ferrar to the *permanent* diaconate at Little Gidding. Ferrar remained a deacon until his death in 1637. His functions were liturgy, word, and charity. Cf. Chadwick, *The Reformation,* pp. 228-229, 422.

and theology, a neglect that continues to be felt in the modern Church. As the laity became better educated and more critical the ministry of the word left much to be desired. Had gifted deacons (and laity) been granted this faculty, preaching would have improved.

The deacon was extraordinary minister of baptism and the Eucharist. For this he needed permission from the pastor or Ordinary. Only in grave necessity could he presume this permission (741). He was ordinary minister of exposition, but he could give benediction only in grave necessity (1274:2). Deacons were entitled to give only those blessings to which they were entitled by law (1174:2). In practice, deacons exercised but few of these minimal and ceremonial functions. Theology and practice were concentrated in the priesthood. The diaconate was to most Catholics a mysterious and shadowy step to "ordination" which meant ordination to the priesthood.

The rite for diaconal ordination in the Roman pontifical emphasizes the deacon's ministry of liturgy and word. There is an interesting trace of the old order when the "archdeacon" is directed to lead ordinands to the bishop. But the prayers and rubrics indicate a ceremonial and temporary role for deacons. Their service of charity is practically confined to prayer and good example. Deacons are compared to Jewish levites and their institution is traced to the appointment of the seven hellenists by the twelve.

Until Vatican II deacons were ordained to an order preparatory to the higher grade of the priesthood: "May they merit by worthy steps to advance through your grace from a lower grade to a higher." [28] If *lex orandi* is *lex credendi* the

---

28. "De Ordinatione Diaconi" in *Manuale Ordinandorum According to the Roman Pontifical,* Beatty, 1917, pp. 48-58.

Church of Rome, until recently, considered the diaconate a preliminary step to the priesthood whose functions were mainly liturgy, word, and the charity of edification. Not surprisingly, recent rituals closely resembled the pontificals in use during the Middle Ages when the diaconate had already declined.

In 1947 Pope Pius XII determined the essential part of the rite for diaconal ordination. The "matter" was the imposition of hands by the ordaining bishop; the "form" was a sentence in the preface.

Now regarding the matter and the form in conferring each individual Order, with Our same Supreme Apostolic Authority, We determine and establish the following: In the Ordination to the Diaconate the matter is the imposition of the Bishop's hand which occurs once in the rite of that Order. And the form consists of these words of the "Preface" which are essential and so required for validity: 'Send forth in him, we beseech you, O Lord, the Holy Spirit to strengthen him by your sevenfold gift of grace that he may faithfully perform the work of your ministry.' [29]

Meanwhile a movement for restoration of the diaconate was underway in Germany. Two priests who had been prisoners at Dachau, Otto Pies and Wilhelm Schamoni, urged the ordination

---

29. Pope Pius XII *Constitutio Apostolica De Sacris Ordinibus Diaconatus, Presbyteratus et Episcopatus,* in *Acta Apostolicae Sedis,* Vol. 40, 1948, pp. 6-7.

of permanent and married deacons.[30] They received enthusiastic support from Josef Hornef, a magistrate, and from "Caritas," a Catholic welfare organization. Their efforts bore fruit in 1951 when the first "Community of the Diaconate" was founded in Freiburg/Breisgau.

Interest soon spread beyond Germany. At an international congress of pastoral liturgy at Assisi in 1956 it became clear the magisterium was listening. Bishop Von Bekkum of Indonesia proposed the possibility of restoration. The question was now an international one.[31]

Pius XII referred to the movement for restoration of the diaconate in his allocution of October 5, 1957. Although he believed "the time is not yet ripe" the Pope was sympathetic. Since Trent there had been debate about the identity of the lower *"ministri"* within the hierarchy. Pius XII added his voice to the majority of theologians who taught the diaconate was hierarchical.[32] The movement for restoration continued to gather momentum. At Holland in 1959 Archbishop d'Souza proposed a married diaconate for all Christian countries.

The idea was debated during the "pre-preparatory" phase preceding Vatican II. A petition for restoration, sponsored by Caritas International, was sent in July, 1959, to all the Council Fathers. The petition resulted in an influential book

---

30. See, for example, Wilhelm Schamoni *Familienvöter als geweihe Diakona*, Paderborn, 1953; *Married Men As Ordained Deacons*, London, 1955; *Ordonner Diacres des Peres de Famille*, Paris, 1961.

31. Committee on the Permanent Diaconate in Canada, "Guidelines of the Episcopal Committee on the Permanent Diaconate," Ottawa, 19-67, pp. 5-6.

32. Pius XII, "Quelques aspects fondamentaux de L'apostolat des laics," *Acta Apostolicae Sedis*, Vol. 49, 1957, pp. 924-925.

by thirty authors from all over the world edited by Karl Rahner.[33] It soon became clear that what was worrying opponents of the restoration was fear of erosion of the discipline of celibacy in the Latin West. But in 1961 the preparatory commission *De Sacramentis,* which included Karl Rahner, responded positively to the numerous *vota* requesting restoration by proposing a permanent diaconate. In the months immediately preceding the convening of the council in 1962 curial opponents maneuvered unsuccessfully to block the proposal.

The proposal came to the floor of the Council during the second session of Vatican II. The question of restoration was debated heatedly by Council Fathers from October 4-16, 1963. Speakers from Central Africa, Thailand, Eastern Europe, Mexico, Argentina, Peru and Brazil favored a permanent diaconate. Cardinals Döpfner and Suenens and then Archbishop Seper spoke impressively for restoration. But there was vigorous opposition from black Africa, the United States, Spain, Italy and Portugal. The Superior General of the Dominicans spoke against restoration, as did Cardinals Ottaviani, Ruffini, Bacci and Spellman. Cardinal Spellman carried his attack to the press. Shrugging off the need for deacons in Latin America the conservative New York prelate said, "The reason I am against it is that it is unnecessary." [34]

But the real *bete noire* of the opposition was optional celibacy.[35] They feared — correctly as it later turned out — that

---

33. *Diaconia in Christo. Uber die Erneverung des Diakonates,* Freiburg, 1962.

34. *The New York Times,* October 5, 1963, p. 1.

35. Xavier Rhynne, *The Second Session,* N.Y., 1964, pp. 101-104, 114. This readable account remains a fine on the spot source for Vatican II. Future historians will consider it a valuable contemporary document.

approval of a married diaconate would open a Pandora's box. Cardinal Suenens met this fear head on by going to the heart of the difficulty. He argued for pluralism; the diaconate would be restored only where regional conferences of bishops approved the restoration. A married diaconate would not be imposed uniformly on the whole Church. The restoration would be motivated wholly by regional pastoral needs.

> All the Council should do is explicitly envisage at least the possibility of such a stable ministry, not for the whole Church, but only for those regions in which (with the consent of the proper authority) the legitimate pastors consider this restoration to be necessary if the Church is not to decline but grow and flourish.[36]

Suenens recommended restoration where small Catholic communities were scattered and, at the opposite end of the spectrum, where urban throngs lacked a sense of community. He countered curial objections that men in minor orders or even laymen could perform diaconal services. The diaconal function, said Suenens, belonged within the official ordering of the church as a hierarchical society. The diaconal task should be performed by those with the necessary charism.

> It is not a matter of giving these external tasks in any way at all or to any one of the faithful . . . these tasks should be given only to him who objectively and adequately has

---

36. Cardinal L. J. Suenens, "The Theology of the Diaconate," in *Council Speeches of Vatican II*, Hans Küng, Yves Congar, Daniel O'Hanlon, eds., Glen Rock, 1964, p. 105.

the necessary graces, so that in building a true community there will be no lack of supernatural efficacy. Unless this is true the Church cannot be a true supernatural society, the true Mystical Body of Christ, built up harmoniously on those ministries and graces which the Lord has foreordained.[37]

On October 21 Cardinal Ottaviani, using his prerogative as a curial Cardinal, attempted to stem the tide by reiterating the curial line that acolytes could perform these functions. But on October 30 progressives pushed through a vote that the schema *De Ecclesia* should deal with restoration of the diaconate *in principal,* postponing for a time the inevitable question of the ordination of married men. The vote for inclusion was 1588 for, 525 against.[38]

The minority, however, was irrepressible. During the interval between the second and third sessions the curial party maneuvered to incorporate into the schema a clause restrict-

---

37. *Ibid.,* p. 104.

38. The backstage maneuverings that preceded this vote almost disrupted the council. The progressive "moderators" in favor of the motion, including Cardinal Suenens, were forced to compromise by deleting specific references to restoration of a *married* diaconate. *That* question was left to surface later. Cf. Xavier Rhynne, *The Second Session,* pp. 164-165, 171. The fateful proposition on the diaconate was phrased as follows with no mention of *married* deacons: "Does it please the Fathers to have the schema declare that the opportuneness should be considered of restoring the diaconate as a distinct and permanent grade of the sacred ministry, according to the needs of the Church in the various areas?" Only the most ingenuous would believe that this delicately phrased proposition does not imply that a *married* clergy was at stake. 1,588 Fathers voted "placet," but 525 voted "non."

ing the admission of married deacons to the Holy See. But the liberating spirit of collegiality was now too prevalent for such regressive centralization. The progressives were willing to reserve to the Pope the right to approve regional proposals for restoration — but the reception of candidates was to depend on local conditions.

When the council reconvened in St. Peter's for the third session the explosive question of the ordination of married men, especially *young* married men, was the key issue where the diaconate was concerned. The third session of the Council would determine the future of the diaconate in the Roman communion.

At the 90th General Congregation, September 29, 1964, with the venerable Cardinal Agagianian in the moderator's chair, the fathers cast their ballots in four separate sections. The revival of the permanent diaconate was approved in principal, 1903 for, 242 against. Local authorities, with Papal approval, could decide on the *actual* restoration in their region, 1523 for, 702 against. The diaconate could be granted to married men of mature age, 1598 for, 629 against. Finally, the proposal that *young* married men could be ordained deacons was defeated, 839 for, 1364 against.[39]

Not without controversy the permanent deacon had returned to the Latin West.

The momentous text of *Lumen Gentium* which signals the return of the deacon reads as follows:

---

39. For an account of the voting see Gerard Philips, "History of the Constitution" in *Commentary on the Documents of Vatican II*, Herbert Vorgrimter, ed., 5 vols., N.Y., 1967, Vol. 1, pp. 116, 130.

At a lower level of the hierarchy are deacons, upon whom hands are imposed 'not unto the priesthood, but unto a ministry of service.' For strengthened by sacramental grace, in communion with the bishop and his group of priests, they serve the People of God in the ministry of the liturgy, of the word, and of charity. It is the duty of the deacon, to the extent that he has been authorized by competent authority, to administer baptism solemnly, to be custodian and dispenser of the Eucharist, to bring Viaticum to the dying, to read the sacred Scripture to the faithful, to instruct and exhort the people, to preside at the worship and prayer of the faithful, to administer sacramentals, and to officiate at funeral and burial services. Dedicated to duties of charity and of administration, let deacons be mindful of the admonition of Blessed Polycarp: 'Be merciful, diligent, walking according to the truth of the Lord, who became the servant of all.'

These duties, so very necessary for the life of the Church, can in many areas be fulfilled only with difficulty according to the prevailing discipline of the Latin Church. For this reason, the diaconate can in the future be restored as a proper and permanent rank of the hierarchy. It pertains to the competent territorial bodies of bishops, of one kind or another, to decide, with the approval of the Supreme Pontiff, whether and where it is opportune for such deacons to be appointed for the care of souls. With the consent of the Roman Pontiff, this diaconate will be able to be conferred upon men of more mature age, even upon those living in the married state. It may also be conferred upon suitable young men. For them, however, the law of celibacy must remain intact.[40]

Deacons, but not other *"ministri,"* are within the hierarchy. The council took care not to offend those few theologians who had taught the diaconate was not sacramental — deacons are "strengthened by sacramental grace." An important development is the assertion that deacons serve "in communion with" bishop and priests, a clear reinterpretation of the "lower rank" theology of the Middle Ages. The deacon's participation in hierarchical priesthood is not conceived in an ascending order; rather, it is understood as descending from Christ through the bishop. The council therefore implies a special role for deacons, the theology of which it leaves open.

The services of deacons are comprehended within their traditional role of liturgy, word, and charity. The specific functions mentioned by the council are not exclusive but are examples of future services permanent deacons will provide. Here we observe that the deacon's ceremonial role at the Eucharist is not emphasized. The council goes far beyond the traditional delimitation of the diaconate to ancillary functions. Deacons are now *ordinary* ministers at baptism and holy communion and even preside at liturgical services. Finally, the emphasis this magisterial text places on charity is significant. Diaconal charity includes administration — deacons may at

---

40. Dogmatic Constitution on the Church in *The Documents of Vatican II,* Walter Abbott ed., N.Y., 1966, chapter III, no. 29, pp. 55-56. Succeeding citations from the Vatican II documents are taken from Abbott.

times free bishops for pastoral service in the midst of God's people. The whole tenor of the restoration is pastoral.

In a subsequent chapter, *Lumen Gentium* again mentions deacons. The traditional "lesser rank" expression reappears, but does not imply an ascending theology of ministry. For deacons are servants of *Christ and the Church,* a pointed expression teaching that they are not merely servants of "higher" ministers. The council noted that this was the expression used by Ignatius of Antioch.

> In their own special way, ministers of lesser rank also share in the mission and grace of the supreme priest. First among these are deacons. Since they are servants of the mysteries of Christ and the Church, they should keep themselves free from every fault, be pleasing to God, and be a source of all goodness in the sight of men (cf. 1 Tm 3:8-10).[41]

In the *Decree on Eastern Catholic Churches* the council urged restoration of the diaconate in the East. This time the council used forceful language — it "ardently desires" the restoration. "In order that the ancient discipline of the sacrament of orders may flourish again in the eastern churches, this sacred synod ardently desires that where it has fallen into disuse the office of the permanent diaconate be restored."[42] Tactfully,

---

41. *Ibid.,* Chapter V, no. 41, p. 69; cf. also Decree on the Bishops Pastoral Office, *Ibid.,* Chapter II, no. 15, p. 406: ". . . deacons are ordained for services and minister *to the people of God in communion with the bishop and his presbytery."* (Italics added)

42. *Decree on Eastern Catholic Churches, Ibid.,* no. 17, p. 380.

the council did not mention that the diaconate had declined in the Eastern Churches partly because of western influence.

Cardinal Suenen's recommendation that men already performing diaconal services should be ordained bore fruit in the decree on the missions.[43] By teaching that these men are to be strengthened by the sacrament and bound more closely to the altar the council again implies a special theology of the diaconate. Referring to *Lumen Gentium,* the decree on missions uses strong language in giving a mandate for restoration; where episcopal conferences deem it opportune "the order of the diaconate should be restored as a permanent state of life."

Where Episcopal Conferences deem it opportune, the order of the diaconate should be restored as a permanent state of life, according to the norms of the Constitution on the Church. For there are men who are actually carrying out the functions of the deacon's office, either by preaching the Word of God as catechists, or by presiding over scattered Christian communities in the name of the pastor and the bishop, or by practicing charity in social or relief work. It will be helpful to strengthen them by that imposition of hands which has come down from the apostles, and to bind them more closely to the altar. Thus they can carry out their ministry more effectively because of the sacramental grace of the diaconate.[44]

---

43. Cardinal L. J. Suenens, "Theology of the Diaconate," in *Council Speeches of Vatican II,* p. 105.

44. Decree on the Missionary Activity of the Church, in *Documents of Vatican II,* chapter II, no. 16, p. 605, *Ibid.*

The *Constitution on the Liturgy*, a document which was promulgated *before* the restoration of the diaconate, recommended presidency by deacons at Bible services of scattered communities, an idea dear to the former Cardinal Montini who was now Pope Paul VI.

Bible services should be encouraged, especially on the vigils of the more solemn feasts, on some weekdays in Advent and Lent, and on Sundays and feast days. They are particularly to be commended in places where no priest is available; when this is so, a deacon or some other person authorized by the bishop should preside over the celebration.[45]

Pope Paul VI returned to this proposal in his instruction on the Constitution; where priests were lacking a deacon or even a layman should preside "at the holy celebration of the word of God." [46]

Another conciliar text, the *Dogmatic Constitution on Divine Revelation*, urged priests, catechists and deacons to diligent study of scripture. The council therefore clearly envisioned a revival of the deacon's ministry of the word. "All the clergy must hold fast to the sacred scriptures through diligent sacred reading and careful study, especially the priests of Christ and others, such as deacons and catechists who are legitimately active in ministry of the word." [47]

---

45. Constitution on the Sacred Liturgy, *Ibid.,* Chapter I, no. 35:4, p. 149.

46. Pope Paul VI, "Instructio ad Executionem Constitutionis de Sacra Liturgia," in *Acta Apostolicae Sedis,* Vol. 56, 1964, pp. 884-885.

47. Dogmatic Constitution on Divine Revelation, in *Documents of Vatican II,* chapter VI, no. 25, p. 127.

During the fourth session the first international congress on the diaconate was held at Rome, October 22-25, 1965. Speakers from various countries discussed reestablishment of the diaconate. Several expositions examined the theology of the diaconate, the formation of deacons, the mission of deacons today, deacons in the missions, in religious orders, and in Latin America.[48]

On December 8, 1965, Pope Paul VI's *"Ite in pace"* rang out in the huge square before St. Peter's. The council was over — and the fathers left the serene embrace of Bernini's colonnades for their flocks throughout the world.

But practical guidelines were still necessary for implementation of the momentous decision to restore the diaconate. There were few experienced experts to consult — for deacons had not flourished in the Latin West for a millennium. Accordingly an international commission, including Bishop Ernest Unterkoefler of Charleston, was established to advise Pope Paul in preparing a detailed *motu proprio* providing guidelines for the actual restoration. It is one thing for a council to decree a dramatic change in the hierarchical ministry; it is another thing to implement this change when recent precedent, especially in the west, is almost wholly lacking.

The Pope and his advisors did their work thoroughly and well. On June 18, 1967, *Sacrum Diaconatus Ordinem* appeared. After citing key conciliar texts on the restoration the Pope observed that it was opportune and necessary for him to provide "certain and definite norms" for the actual resto-

-----

48. The main contributions were published in *Le diacre dans l'Eglise* along with several essays from *Diaconia in Christo*.

ration.[49] After stating that existing Canon Law, unless otherwise determined, remained in effect, the Pope listed no less than thirty six "certain and definite norms" as guidelines for the actual restoration.

Regional episcopal conferences are to decide, with the approval of the Holy See, whether or not the permanent diaconate shall be actually restored in their regions. In petitioning for restoration they are to indicate the reasons for their proposal and the manner in which restoration will proceed. If approbation is forthcoming the local ordinary is responsible for the selection and ordination of candidates within his jurisdiction. In his periodic reports to Rome he is to include the status of the diaconate in his diocese (I).

The diaconate may be conferred on men twenty five years of age or older. Young men are bound to celibacy. They are to reside for a time in a designated college of formation. Bishops of a region should cooperate in choosing the location and directors of formation. Young men are to pursue a three year course in doctrinal, spiritual, and pastoral formation (II).

Married men of "mature years" (thirty five) may be admitted to the diaconate. The consent of their wives is necessary; wives must be women who will not object to their husband's ministry. Married candidates shall be virtuous men who are successful husbands and fathers. Older men, whether married or single, shall reside "for some time" in a college of formation. In exceptional circumstances they may receive their training from a carefully chosen priest. Deacons must work in

---

49. Pope Paul VI, "Sacrum Diaconatus Ordinem," in *Acta Apostolicae Sedis*, Vol. 59, 1967, pp. 697-704.

professions suitable to their role in the Church. After ordination unmarried deacons are obliged to celibacy (III).

Every deacon, unless he is a religious, shall be incorporated in a diocese. Episcopal conferences will decide on appropriate financial provision for deacons and, if they are married, for their families. When possible deacons should contribute to their own support (IV).

As specified in the *Dogmatic Constitution on the Church* the deacon, with the Ordinary's approval, is to perform the liturgical functions proper to his order, to administer solemn baptism and to supply omitted ceremonies, to reserve and distribute the Eucharist and viaticum, to give benediction with the pax, to assist at and bless marriages if a priest is not available, to administer sacramentals, to preside at funerals and burials, to preach, to read scripture in church, to preside at prayer when a priest is not available, to preside at Bible services, to administer charity in the name of the hierarchy, to lead scattered communities in the name of the pastor and bishop, to assist the ministry of the laity. These services are rendered to God's people and the world in perfect communion with the bishop and priests. Here the *motu proprio* makes clear that deacons are "under the authority of the bishop *and priest* who are responsible for the care of souls in a place." Deacons are to participate, if possible, in pastoral councils (V).

Because of their order deacons are to excel in liturgy, prayer, charity, chastity, obedience, and the ministry. Episcopal conferences shall determine norms for strengthening the spiritual life of deacons. The ordinary must take care that his deacons faithfully read and meditate on the word of God, frequently receive the Eucharist and Penance, and venerate and love the

Mother of God. It is recommended that permanent deacons read part of the Divine office. They should make a retreat at least every third year. Deacons are to continue their study so that they can skillfully explain Catholic doctrine. They should receive periodic in-service training. Deacons owe peculiar obedience to their bishop who, in turn, has a warm paternal love for them. If a deacon is compelled to live in another diocese he is subject to the local ordinary in all that pertains to the diaconate. He shall dress according to the norms to be decided by regional episcopal conferences (VI).

The Holy See reserves the right to constitute a permanent diaconate among religious in cooperation with general chapters. Religious deacons are subject to ecclesiastical superiors according to the norms of religious priests. They are bound by the constitutions of their religious community. When a religious deacon resides in a diocese where the diaconate has yet to be restored he is not to function without the express approval of the local Ordinary. The norms for religious deacons apply to other communities which profess the counsels (VII).

The present Ordinal remains in effect for the ordination of deacons until the Holy See approves a revised rite. The *motu proprio* concludes by proposing the examples of Stephen of Jerusalem and Lawrence, deacon of Rome. The document was promulgated at the Eternal City on the feast of St. Ephraem, deacon of Syria (VIII).

Considering the long and silent centuries in which the ministry of service had been in eclipse the detailed and far-sighted *motu proprio* was an amazing accomplishment. Through the instant communications unknown to the deacons of history the document reached the New World in June, 1967. The

American bishops studied the papal guidelines — and decided to act.

In April, 1968, the National Conference of Catholic Bishops adopted as their own a Position Paper on the diaconate, closely adhering to the *motu proprio,* prepared by an *Ad Hoc* committee.[50] They formally petitioned the Holy See for the restoration of the diaconate in the United States.

Four months later the NCCB received from the Vatican an affirmative reply to their petition. In the United States, for the permanent diaconate all systems were "go."

Bishop Joseph L. Bernardin, general secretary of the NCCB, announced to the American public the Vatican's approval of a permanent diaconate in the United States. On the recommendation of the Vatican Congregation of the Sacraments Pope Paul VI provided:

1. that with the consent of the local bishop the diaconate can be restored where needed;
2. that it can be conferred on married or unmarried men "of mature years";
3. that married deacons, if their wife dies, cannot remarry;
4. that unmarried deacons cannot marry;
5. that unmarried men of twenty five years or older are eligible for the diaconate;
6. that at least a two year program of training before ordination to the diaconate is suggested.[51]

---

50. "A Proposal Paper on the Permanent Diaconate Presented to the National Conference of Catholic Bishops." Unpublished paper.

51. "Conditions for Permanent Diaconate in United States," in *The Catholic Mind,* Vol. LXVI, no. 1227, November, 1968, p. 8.

The NCCB decided that for an experimental period the diaconate will be conferred on married or single men thirty five years of age or older. In November, 1968, a Standing Committee on the Permanent Diaconate was established. This important committee consists of five bishops, four priest consultants, and four deacons. The function of the committee is to guide and expedite, according to the guidelines of the *motu proprio* and NCCB Position Paper, the restoration of the diaconate in the United States. Local bishops are responsible for the diaconate in their dioceses with the proviso that local programs are approved by the Standing Committee.

As these words are written permanent deacons are returning to the ministry where they now serve God's people in communion with bishops and priests. National training programs are preparing deacons at St. John's University, Collegeville, Minnesota, and the National Polish Seminary at Orchard Lake, Michigan. Local programs for "part time" as well as "full time" permanent deacons are operative in such pioneering dioceses as Detroit, Hartford, Cleveland, Chicago and dozens more.

Candidates from every walk of life, rich and poor, married and single, middle aged and old, are assuming the diaconal functions so nobly performed by Basil, Lawrence, Ephraem, Francis and thousands more.[52] Catholic Christians and all men of good will can be grateful for a radically new agency of human reconciliation as the deacon returns.

---

52. Edward P. Echlin, "The Deacon in the Secular Age," *Worship*, vol. 43, no. 3, March 1969, pp. 157-158.

Epilogue:
The Future Deacon

"I say, as do all Christian men, that it is a Divine Purpose that rules, and not fate."

Alfred the Great

We have observed that the historic reality of the diaconate has been liturgy, word and charity in communion with other church officers. Within this same comprehensive context the future deacon will reach out to God's people and the world in continuity with the deacon of yesterday.

But it would be a mistake to expect to find in some golden age of the past a perfect blueprint for the future diaconate. There *is* a reality to the triadic ministry that should be maintained — but within that reality the role of the future deacon will develop. Just as the early Church ordered itself to include permanent deacons and later let the diaconate decline, so the modern Church has restored the diaconate. There is therefore a pluralism in the diaconate, pluralism in the present, pluralism with the past, and with the future. While the services of tomorrow's deacon will be continuous with the ministry of past deacons, they will also be radically different. The deacon has returned to his ministry to meet the unprecedented needs of alienated societies in a world where instant communications have telescoped the universe, where technocratic

127

societies fear the future, and where the Church is groping for a key to unlock the door that bars the Church from relevance to the world.

The bishops of the world, gathered in council, restored the permanent diaconal functions of liturgy, word and charity. But the bishops endorsed the openness of an uncharted future for the diaconal ministry; the deacon's role will be discerned and delineated as it develops in response to tomorrow's needs.[1]

The dramatic return of the deacon coincides with the agonized yearning of the wounded giant that is the Roman Catholic Church to break out of isolation and serve the world. The deacon's return, while coincidental with the Church's outreach to modern man, is no coincidence. With warm pastoral concern, Vatican II addressed the world on behalf of all God's people.

> This sacred Synod proclaims the highest destiny of man and champions the godlike seed which has been sown in him. It offers to mankind the honest assistance of the Church in fostering that brotherhood of all men which corresponds to this destiny of theirs. Inspired by no earthly ambition, the Church seeks but a solitary goal: to carry forward the work of Christ Himself under the lead of the befriending Spirit. And Christ entered this world to give witness to the truth, to rescue and not to sit in judgment, to serve and not to be served.[2]

---

1. Edward P. Echlin, "The Origins of the Permanent Deacon," *American Ecclesiastical Review,* August, 1970, pp. 92-94.

2. Pastoral Constitution on the Church in the Modern World, *Documents of Vatican II,* Preface, no. 4, p. 202.

To assist mankind, to foster brotherhood, to carry forth the work of Christ, to give witness to truth, to rescue, to serve — this goal of the Church in the modern world makes a reordering of the Church imperative. The Church has responded by restoring the diaconate.

In his person the deacon is a living sign, a light to the nations, of the Church's concern for mankind. We suggest that the role of the future deacon will be that of *intermediary*. The deacon bridges sacred worship and secular worship, horizontal prayer and vertical prayer, the bread of the Eucharist and the bread of practical charity. In his service to the world the deacon proclaims and witnesses to the reconciliation of all men in Christ. In his charity the deacon brings to men more than the bread the necessary welfare agencies bring, he brings to men bread leavened with the Christian concern for persons that nourishes man's self as well as man's body. The deacon reads the signs of the times and mediates the needs and concerns of men to bishops, presbyters and laity so that the Church can focus its mission and message where reconciliation is most desperately needed. The deacon is an intermediary between Church and world, world and Church, between the hierarchy and all mankind, between mankind and the hierarchy.

Through the deacon the priesthood is grounded in the midst of the human family. The deacon, no less than other ministers, shares in Christ's priesthood. But in a special way he is Christ the servant washing the wounded feet of mankind. In suffering men the deacon, who represents the servant Christ, finds Christ in the least of his brethren. Through the deacon the Christian hierarchy of service mediates eucharistic love to mankind.

The signs of the times are revolutionary. The Johannine Church opened its windows only to find itself in a time of revolution without a structure to cope with revolution. Revolution is a word freighted with connotations of violence and irrationality, yet in a true sense the Church itself is an agent of revolution. Christian revolution is *reconciliation,* the politics of eschatological hope in society.[3] The Church, content with no status quo, surges forward as a preparatory sign of future reconciliation when all men in Christ will live as brothers. The deacon, as intermediary between the Church, and the hopes, the joys, and the anxieties of men, is a leader of God's people in the revolutionary mission of reconciliation.

In the reordered ministry of bishop, priest and deacon, the Roman Catholic Church has restructured itself for revolution. The future deacon will bring to bear on the human family the eschatological unity celebrated in Christian worship, he will lead God's people to the sore spots in nature and history where Christian unity and the Christian word are most desperately needed.

In his ministry he will cooperate with Catholic priests. When the diaconate was conceived as a lower grade in an ascending hierarchy there was anxiety in "higher" ministers to keep the deacon in his place. But when the deacon is correctly understood as an intermediary who serves in communion with other ministers the disedifying spectre of friction within the ministry should vanish. The deacon's role is not "lower than" nor "inferior to" the priest's, he is not a potential rival; his charism

---

3. Carl E. Braten, *The Future of God,* N.Y., 1969, pp. 142-166.

is *different* than any other charism in the Church including that of the priest. The deacon serves in liturgy and charity *in communion with* other ministers. The future deacon will *assist* the priest with whom he serves. With the assistance of the deacon as intermediary the priest's ministry of teaching, guiding and sanctifying will be responsive to human needs.

Nevertheless the return of the deacon may have unsettling repercussions on the life of the priest. Since the third century priests have often preempted functions appropriate to deacons and laity. In America the parish priest sometimes became all things to all men. When America urbanized, specialized, and went to college the priest found his functions siphoned off one at a time by a progressively better educated laity. No longer was he the best equipped social worker, teacher, counsellor, administrator, coach, lector, or even preacher in an area. Yet his familiar role as an activist among activists was so deeply ingrained that the priest of the secular age eventually found himself in a confused and, until people got over the shock, disedifying identity crisis.

The return of the deacon has brought the identity crisis in the priesthood to a head. We suggest here that the kairotic and evangelical role of the future priest may be discerned by meditation on the appointment of the seven hellenist "deacons" by the twelve apostles. We are contending that the role of the priest is that of the twelve and *not* that of the seven (service at tables); the special charism of the priest is prayer and ministry of the word. The future deacon, whose own ministry of the word is primarily introductory and rudimentary, will liberate priests from "administration" and "men for others" activism so that they can devote themselves to prayer, study, and effective preaching. Through renewed preaching by priests all Christians may be inspired to a deeper self-understanding of the church as a revolutionary community of reconciliation, a preparatory sign of the reign of God.

After a lapse of centuries in the Latin West the permanent deacon once again brings marriage to the ministry. Here too the deacon is an intermediary; in his person he combines marriage and the ministry. Just as there will always be a need for celibacy in the ministry, so too there is a need for *marriage* in the ministry. The minister who shares life with a woman brings to the ministry a dimension that enriches the witness of celibate deacons and priests. In married deacons God's people will be served by ministers who share the totality of the human condition including the option to participate in the cost and fulfillment of indefinite commitment to a person.

The married ministry will bring novel problems to Roman Catholicism, problems not encountered where celibacy has been the law for a long and lonely millennium. But the problems of a married (and therefore pluralist) ministry are far more human and far less costly to persons than the perennial and irrepressible problems endemic to compulsory celibacy. The curial party which opposed restoration of the diaconate at Vatican II was correct — as conservatives so often are correct. The married diaconate is the penultimate step to a married priesthood. The deacon already performs a reconciling service as he hastens the day when all Christian men, including those who wish to serve God's people as priests, will be free to marry or not marry for the kingdom of heaven. Only when married priests are welcomed to Catholic ministry will the celibate priest be seen as a wholly free man.

The revival of the married diaconate also raises the question of the ordination of women. There is abundant historical precedent for orders of deaconesses. We have noticed how deaconesses were taken for granted in the formative centuries of the Church. By the eighth century the female diaconate had almost wholly declined in the west and soon after fell into disuse even in the East. Thereafter religious women have performed female diaconal functions.

Today when the Spirit moves in the Church to bring men and women together,[4] we propose that women should be readmitted to the diaconate. Existing programs for the formation of deacons can and should be extended to admit and train women candidates. When women share unambiguously the diaconate, Catholic ministry will fully represent and therefore fully serve the human condition.[5]

We repeat that there is no golden age in the dim past which, once rediscovered, will provide a blueprint for tomorrow's diaconate. Even *if* the deaconesses of the past were less than fully "ordained" into the ministry this precedent does not prohibit God's people from opening the future diaconate to women. The restored diaconate is itself a reminder that the Catholic triadic ministry is not the only apostolic ministry the Church

---

4. Eugene Kennedy, *Fashion Me a People*, N.Y., 1967, pp. 37-51; 93-109.

5. Agnes Cunningham, "The Ministry of Women in the Church," *Proceedings of the Catholic Theological Society of America*, Yonkers, 1969, pp. 139-141.

has known.[6] Just as the Church under the Spirit let the diaconate decline and later restored it, so the Church could return to a primitive charismatic ordering such as existed in the Pauline churches or develop a totally unprecedented ministry in the future. It is not clear that there is any divine law preventing the Church from admitting women to the diaconate. On the contrary the Spirit may well be urging God's people to recognize the diaconal services of women. We do well to remind ourselves that if it is true that no one can love quite like a woman, it is equally true that no one can serve quite like a woman. Only when women are welcomed to the diaconate will the ministry of service be itself fully reconciled to the wholeness of humanity. Only when women ministers serve with men as equal partners will the diaconate be wholly apt for reconciliation of *all* human needs.

The deacon (and deaconess) of the future will be before all else a builder of human community. Never has the human family been so enslaved to the machine — and never before have men so audibly yearned for community. As the Church's intermediary the deacon will anoint and bring viaticum to the dying. He will extend the embrace of Christian community to the aged. He will bring a sense of belonging to the incarcerated, the mentally ill, the handicapped, the blind, and all God's children whenever they are lonely. The deacon will serve migrant and rural families. He will unify and lead scattered Christian communities. He will strive to humanize sprawling universities and impersonal urban parishes. As coordinator of

---

6. Echlin, "The Origins of the Permanent Deacon," *American Ecclesiastical Review,* pp. 83-86.

religious education the deacon will be a center of community in the parish.

The agonized search for small communities in technocratic America is an amazing sign of the times which the future deacon must discern. He will strive to liberate urban men from the shallow "necessities" conjured up by advertizing. By organizing God's people to lobby for public transportation the deacon will liberate men from the horrible tyranny of the automobile. Where community is in the process of taking hold the deacon will foster it; where community is lacking he will serve through liturgy, word, and charity as a catalyst of unification. The deacon will discern the movement now sweeping through the Church for new, ecumenical and heterosexual forms of religious life. As intermediary he will report these yearnings to the bishop. By aiding men and women to love one another the deacon will himself be a great sign by which all men will know God's people are Christ's disciples.

The demands on tomorrow's deacon will transcend the needs for service that confronted the deacons of yesterday. The Church in technological societies must share its skills, its wealth and its word with underdeveloped nations — and warn young nations against the dehumanization that industrialization can bring. The deacon, who has ever been administrator of the church's charity, is uniquely fitted to lead God's people in sharing with the third world.

A final unprecedented challenge for the future deacon is the service of reconciliation of man and man's environment. The Church has been woefully slow in exerting leadership in the environmental crisis that is perhaps the gravest crisis ever to threaten the human family. The deacon will teach reverence for the earth, he will teach that man and history are not set off from a devalued nature, but that in Christ man, nature and history form a redeemed unity. Nature too has inherent value; nature too is destined for the reign of God. As the Church's paramount revolutionary the future deacon must take a lead in reconciling man and the universe.

In conclusion, the long and varied biography of the deacon turns a new corner with the timely restoration of the permanent diaconate. The deacon may provide the answer to the widening challenge that for years has stymied all Christians, young and old, progressive and conservative, Roman and non-Roman — how can we, God's people, reconcile men in this their hour of gravest need? As his role develops within the context of liturgy, word, and charity the deacon may find the key — indeed he may *be* the key — that will open not windows but the doors that divide the Church from the world. The world craves reconciliation. The Church's mission is reconciliation. The deacon is the ordained intermediary of reconciliation.

May Christians and all men of good will extend a warm welcome to this new yet old ministry as the deacon returns.

Bibliography

"Conditions for Permanent Diaconate in U.S." *The Catholic Mind,* November, 1968, p. 55.

J. P. Audet, *Structures of Christian Priesthood,* N.Y., 1967.

Roger Beckwith, "Office of Women in the Church, to the Present Day," *Churchman,* April 1969, pp. 170-183.

Raymond E. Brown, *Priest and Bishop,* N. Y., 1970.

Alex J. Brunett, *The Permanent Diaconate,* Detroit, 1970.

Committee on the Permanent Diaconate in Canada, "Guidelines of the Episcopal Committee on the Permanent Diaconate," Ottawa, 1967.

Agnes Cunningham, "The Ministry of Women in the Church," *Proceedings of the Catholic Theological Society of America,* Yonkers, 1969.

Jean Danielou, *The Ministry of Women in the Early Church,* London, 1961.

Edward P. Echlin, "The Origins of the Permanent Deacon," *The American Ecclesiastical Review,* August, 1970, pp. 92-106.

Jean Guyot (ed.), *The Sacrament of Holy Orders,* London, 1962.

Josef Hornef, *The New Vocation,* London, 1963.

"El Diaconado Como Estado Permanente," *Concilium*

(Espana), 4, 1968, pp. 277-286.

Hans Küng, *The Church*, London, 1967.

Council Speeches of Vatican II, Glen Rock, 1964.

J. I. McCord and T. H. L. Parker (eds.), *Service in Christ*, Grand Rapids, 1966.

John L. McKenzie, *Authority in the Church*, N.Y., 1966.

Kevin McNamara (ed.), *Vatican II: The Constitution on the Church*, London, 1968.

James A. Mohler, *The Origin and Evolution of the Priesthood*, Alba House, Staten Island, N.Y., 1970.

Richard Nolan (ed.), *The Diaconate Now*, Cleveland, 1968.

Robert Nowell, *The Ministry of Service*, London, 1968.

Karl Rahner & Herbert Vorqrimler, (eds.), *Diakonia in Christo: Uber Die Erneuerung des Diakonates*, Freiburg, 1962.

Wilhelm Schamoni, *Married Men as Ordained Deacons*, London, 1955.

E. Schillebeeckx, *Celibacy*, N.Y., 1968.

"Catholic Understanding of Office," *Theological Studies*, December, 1969, pp. 567-589.

Russell Shaw, *Permanent Deacons, Who, What, and Why*, Washington, 1969.

Gerald Sloyan, "Meanings & Qualities of Ministry — the Office of the Permanent Deacon," in *Living Worship*, September, 1969, pp. 1-6.

L. J. Suenens, *Coresponsibility in the Church*, London, 1968.

Donald F. Thomas, *The Deacon in a Changing Church*, Valley Forge, 1969.

Lukas Visher, *The Ministry of Deacons*, Geneva, 1965.

P. Winninger, *Les Diacres: Histoire et Avenir du Diaconat*, Paris, 1967.

P. Winninger & Y. Congar (eds.), *Le Diacre Dans L'Eglise et le Monde D'Aujourd'hui,* Paris, 1966.

Richard E. Zenk, *The Office of Deacon in Ecclesiastical Law,* Rome, 1969.

Note: A detailed bibliography on the diaconate for the years 1966-1969, including English and Spanish titles, may be obtained from Office National Du Clerge 4635; rue Delorimier; Montreal, Canada.